JANE COOPER

UNDER DISCUSSION
Marilyn Hacker and Kazim Ali, General Editors
Donald Hall, Founding Editor

Volumes in the Under Discussion series collect reviews and essays about individual poets. The series is concerned with contemporary American and English poets about whom the consensus has not yet been formed and the final vote has not been taken. Titles in the series include:

Jane Cooper

A Radiance of Attention

Martha Collins and Celia Bland

Editors

UNIVERSITY OF MICHIGAN PRESS

Ann Arbor

Copyright © 2019 by Martha Collins and Celia Bland

Published in the United States of America by the
University of Michigan Press
Printed and bound by CPI Group (UK) Ltd, Croydon, CR0 4YY

First published April 2019

A CIP catalog record for this book is available from the British Library.
Library of Congress Cataloging-in-Publication data has been applied for.
ISBN 978-0-472-03741-4 (paper : alk. paper)
ISBN 978-0-472-12529-6 (e-book)

Contents

Digital materials related to this title can be found on
the Fulcrum platform via the following citable URL:
https://doi.org/10.3998/mpub.10155814

Acknowledgments

Thanks to W.W. Norton for permission to quote poems and excerpts from *The Flashboat: Poems Collected and Reclaimed* by Jane Cooper. Copyright © 2000 by Jane Cooper. Used by permission of W.W. Norton & Company, Inc.

Our thanks as well to Kazim Ali for supporting this project from the beginning; to the New York Public Library for access to Jane Cooper's papers; to Annie Wright for permission to publish James Wright's previously unpublished review of *The Weather of Six Mornings;* and to Bobbie Kinnell for permission to publish Galway Kinnell's introduction to the Poets House Tribute to Jane Cooper, Donnell Library, October 13, 1994.

Some of these essays, including four that were written as reviews and two that were written for this volume, were previously published. Grateful acknowledgment is given for permission to reprint:

REVIEWS:

Pamela Alexander, "A Boat to See by, a Life to Row," *FIELD* 62 (Spring 2000), 63–73. [review of *The Flashboat*]

Rachel Hadas, from "An Ecstasy of Space," *Parnassus* 15, no. 1 (1989), 217–31. [review of 1984 edition of *Scaffolding*]

David Rigsbee, review of *The Flashboat*, *The Brooklyn Rail* (May 2001), 22.

Lisa Sack, "Angle of Repose: Jane Cooper's Long View," *Voice Literary Supplement* (February 1995), 27. [review of 1993 edition of *Scaffolding* and *Green Notebook, Winter Road*]

ESSAYS:

Kazim Ali, "From the Open Sea: Body and Lyric in the Poetry of Jane Cooper," *Orange Alert* (Ann Arbor: University of Michigan Press, 2010), 5–24.

Celia Bland, "Ordinary Details: Humor in the Work of Jane Cooper," *Rain Taxi Review* 20, no. 2 (Summer 2015), 32–33. [written for this volume]

Eve Grubin, "Jane Cooper and the Poetics of Sanity," *American Poetry Review* 45, no. 4 (July/August 2016), 27. [written for this volume]

Jane Cooper Symposium, *FIELD* 79 (Fall 2008): Essays by the following, under the titles given in this volume: Jan Heller Levi (11–17), Marie Howe (18–20), Philip Levine (21–23), Jean Valentine (24–28), and Thomas Lux (29–31).

CELIA BLAND AND MARTHA COLLINS

Introduction

I'm trying to write a poem that will alert me to my real life,

. . . .

And yet this poem too must allow for the unseen.

("Ordinary Detail" 174)[1]

It is relatively easy to reduce Jane Marvel Cooper's life to its "ordinary details." She was born in Atlantic City, New Jersey, on October 9, 1924, and she died in Newtown, Pennsylvania, on October 26, 2007. The life lived between these two Octobers was one of often unseen but sustained efforts and an always "radiant attention" lavished upon poetry, essays, her friends—"my estate"—and students.

Cooper spent much of her childhood in Jacksonville, Florida. The Coopers were proud of their roles in American history. One Cooper was a hero of the Revolutionary War; another fought with Andrew Jackson in the Seminole Wars against Osceola. Her uncle, Merian C. Cooper (memorialized in her poem "Seventeen Questions About King Kong"), was an anthropologist, aviator, and film producer who, as a young pilot in 1918, was captured by the Red Army in Poland and interrogated by Isaac Babel. Her father, John Cobb Cooper, was known as "the father of Air Space Law"; he advised presidents on the legal niceties of aviation and air space, while her mother, Martha Marvel, raised Cooper and her younger brother and sister in Florida and, later, Princeton, New Jersey.

Young Jane suffered from an inherited immune deficiency and was not expected to live past childhood. Her Scottish nurse tended her until she was five, when her desperate mother took her to New York's Children's Hospital, where Cooper slowly recovered her health. ("I had my life given back," as she put it.) She was never completely well, but she possessed resilience and carefully meted out her energies over a long, productive life.

Cooper spent two years at Vassar College before illness prompted a break in her studies; she eventually graduated in 1946 from the University of Wisconsin-Madison. Inspired by the poetry of Muriel

Rukeyser, she had begun writing in high school and continued to do so during her undergraduate years and then at Oxford, where she studied in 1947 after touring a devastated post-war Europe. She began teaching literature and fiction writing at Sarah Lawrence College in 1950, and took a leave two years later to attend the Writers' Workshop at the University of Iowa. There, studying with John Berryman and Robert Lowell, she met poets Philip Levine and Shirley Eliason Haupt (the latter primarily a visual artist)—friends who inspired her for the rest of her life.

Back at Sarah Lawrence and now teaching poetry, Cooper was in her mid-forties when her first book, *The Weather of Six Mornings,* was named the 1969 Lamont Poetry Selection of the Academy of American Poets, chosen by James Wright (who became a lifelong champion of her work), Hayden Carruth, William Stafford, Donald Hall, and Donald Justice, heavyweights of the (almost exclusively male) poetry world. Her second book, *Maps & Windows* (1974), included poems "reclaimed" from the 1940s and '50s. *Scaffolding: Selected Poems,* published in Britain in 1984 and in the United States in 1993 (the latter when she was sixty), contained sixty short poems from the previous volumes (arranged chronologically, giving "a sense of the continuous journey the work has been for me all along"); one long poem, "Threads: Rosa Luxemburg from Prison," which had first appeared as a chapbook; and an essay about her own work and process, its title paraphrased from a sign glimpsed in post-war Paris: "Nothing Has Been Used in the Manufacture of This Poetry That Could Have Been Used in the Manufacture of Bread." Grace Paley described this book as revealing "a great deep patience for the whole truth, a waiting in quietness for tremor and explosion."

Green Notebook, Winter Road appeared as Cooper turned seventy in 1974. Reflecting upon what she described as an "urgency to explore a woman's consciousness," this collection burrows into the artistic lives of Willa Cather and Georgia O'Keefe, while meditating upon Cooper's own vocation. Other poems treat the topic of illness, and others reconsider what Cooper called "my sensuous, precious, upper-class, / unjust white child's past" (190).

Cooper's last published book, *The Flashboat: Poems Collected and Reclaimed* (1999), contains poems "reclaimed" or resurrected from her past and "reinserted" into the chronology of published work. This volume introduced Cooper's poetry to a younger generation and brought her recognition and acclaim.

A celebrated mentor and teacher—Sarah Lawrence faculty habitually advised students to take a workshop with "Jane" before they graduated—Cooper nurtured the talents of many women writers, including, among many others, Alice Walker, Jan Heller Levi, and Marie Howe. She retired from teaching in 1987, after nearly forty years.

Already the recipient of fellowships from the Guggenheim Foundation, the National Endowment for the Arts, and the Bunting Institute at Radcliffe, as well as the Maurice English Award and the American Academy of Arts and Letters Award, Cooper served as New York State Poet from 1995 to 1997. (Illness necessitated that Grace Paley accept the award in her stead.) She also edited *Extended Outlooks: The Iowa Review Collection of Contemporary Women Writers* (1982) and *The Sanity of Earth and Grass: Complete Poems of Robert Winner* (1994).

Critical appreciation grew with the publication of each of Cooper's collections. She may have deemed herself a "minor" poet, but she was more accurately, perhaps, a poet's poet, revered for her work's honesty, lyric intensity, and emotional precision. Her poetic life followed Willa Cather's maxim (as quoted in "Vocation: A Life"): "Artistic growth is, more than it is anything else, a refining of the sense of truthfulness. . . . [O]nly the artist, the great artist, knows how difficult it is."

In 2007, Jane Cooper died from complications stemming from Parkinson's disease. Her poem "Threads: Rosa Luxemburg in Prison" describes a spirit freed from a cell, a room, from the box of the body; it might serve as her epitaph:

> Thus passing out of my cell in all directions
> are fine threads connecting me
> with thousands of birds and beasts
>> You too . . . are one of this urgent company
>> To which my heart throbs, responsive . . .
>
> (167)

Celia Bland

As suggested above and as noted throughout this collection, a chronological treatment of Jane Cooper's work is challenging. Her earliest poems appeared only in her second collection; both her second and third books rearranged, omitted, reprinted, and "reclaimed" earlier poems, even as they added new ones; and her fifth volume, *The Flashboat: Poems Collected and Reclaimed,* continued the process of omitting, rearranging, and reclaiming. As she notes in the foreword, that final book is "a record of my life in poetry as that record has gone out into the world. If the original self-definitions have been subject to some redefinition, that is part of a lifelong effort to be more honest, to understand a fluid nature in the grip of a difficult century" (19).

In our own difficult century, it seemed important to us to follow that fluid process as closely as possible in the presentation of the essays in this volume. Following an overview by Kazim Ali that looks back at early poems and moves forward into much of the later work, we begin our chronology with Stephen Tapscott's essay on Cooper's earliest poems, which were not in fact published until her second book.

From there, we make some attempt to treat the volumes in the chronological order in which they were published, starting in each case with reviews, moving to general discussions, and ending with essays that deal with individual poems from the relevant volume. Six pieces, beginning with James Wright's previously unpublished review, focus on *The Weather of Six Mornings* (1969) and individual poems from that collection, ending with Eric Gudas's discussion of poems from the same period that were omitted and later "reclaimed." The next three pieces, including two substantial essays that highlight the transition from earlier work, explore *Maps & Windows* (1974); the four after that, beginning with a review by Rachel Hadas, discuss *Scaffolding* (1984) and individual poems from that volume. A brief interlude of three appreciations of Jane Cooper as colleague, teacher, and mentor somewhat interrupts our chronology, which resumes in the next eight pieces, all of which (beginning with Lisa Sack's review) focus on Cooper's fourth book, *Green Notebook, Winter Road* (1994). Two general essays about Cooper, both leaning toward the later work, and two reviews of *The Flashboat* (2000) follow. The volume closes with L. R. Berger's moving tribute to Cooper's final days.

Even as this volume concerns itself with Jane Cooper's complex process of writing, revising, and compiling collections, it contains a remarkable number of essays that discuss single poems. A few of these are reprinted from a symposium published in *FIELD* magazine in 2008, for which writers were asked to write about a single poem; but a number of people who wrote specifically for this volume also chose to focus on individual works. These two approaches to Cooper's writing—attention to a process that involved a great deal of change, and careful examination of well-crafted individual poems—reflect what may seem to be contrasting impulses in Cooper's own work, as suggested by two kinds of metaphors that are mentioned in several of the essays: on the one hand, the body, as in a changing body of work but also the human, and specifically female, body; on the other, architecture, as in Lee Upton's discussion of "The Builder of Houses." But while the organic might seem to stand in contrast if not contradiction to the structural, the two directions stem from the same complex concern. It is, after all, the scaffolding of the building process that Cooper referenced in the title of her third book, not the finished house or building itself; and if she was a painstakingly meticulous constructor of poems, relentless revision was always central to that process.

Another pair of what might be seen as complementary opposites appears in the introduction to *The Flashboat* and suggests what makes Jane Cooper's ever-changing art so ultimately enduring. "Mystery and clarity: these have been my concerns from the beginning. The mystery of our existence on earth. The clarity of a moment's elucidation which is the poem" (20). Clarity may be what first impresses readers of Jane Cooper's poems; mystery is what keeps us returning to them again and again, experiencing them more deeply on each visit.

Martha Collins

Note

1. Jane Cooper, *The Flashboat: Poems Collected and Reclaimed* (New York: Norton, 2000). Since the vast majority of quotations that appear in this anthology come from *The Flashboat*, subsequent quotations from that volume will be identified by page number in parentheses, both here and in the essays that follow.

KAZIM ALI

From the Open Sea
Body and Lyric in the Poetry of Jane Cooper

I met Jane Cooper once in my life, white light of the afternoon pouring through the windows of her Upper West Side apartment. It was late afternoon, spring of 2001, and the sound of the earth moving beneath us seemed at last obvious. Jane moved very deliberately, making our tea, performing each activity: opening the cupboard, taking out cups, pouring water into the kettle. Not one thing was a hinge moment, a transition from one thing to another, at no moment was Jane performing two tasks at once; each moment belonged to itself.

Which is to say, when she looked at me, she looked at me. When she spoke to me, she spoke to me. The space between two figures in the painting in her hallway, the space between the word she spoke and when I heard it and then the next word. Her body existed in that room, in that space, at the beginning of another era in our history; but that moment it still seemed we might move toward peace, might move away from what now seems an inevitably impending endless war.

In her prose poem "The Past," Jane writes of being treated as a child by a doctor whose uncle fought in the war of 1812. The poem concludes, "And how do I connect in my own body—that is, through touch—the War of 1812 with the smart rocket nosing its way via CNN down a Baghdad street? How much can two arms hold? How soon will my body, which already spans a couple of centuries, become almost transparent and begin to shiver apart?" (202).

Cooper held the mortal moment—the moment of the body's failure—as close as she held the breath in the heart of her poems. In between her poems' lines was that pause of silence between one thing and another, a moment that acknowledged bodies' separation from one another, the compassion they owed one another as mortal objects. This mere recognition of compassion seems so important in

6

the present moment, a compassion that requires a principled opposition to all violence and war, a commitment to work toward other solutions.

By the end of her life, of course, Cooper's body would—like all of ours eventually—shiver apart, like a treasure of the earth, dispersing its passions to those connected to her only briefly—including me, a lonely schoolteacher who knew very few poets at all, writing to her out of the blue, in need of hearing any news at all of the earth's survival, anything at all. If in a hundred years future generations want to know what it *felt* like to be alive and human through war, bomb tests, genetic engineering of the food supply, and the dehumanization inherent in the spread of global capital and its attendant de-democratized national and supernational political institutions, one can only pray that among the poems in the time capsule are hers.

It's a panic, I admit—that the individual's body doesn't mean anything in the face of the machinations of the state and the corporation. That to *be* an individual at all, with one's own perceptions, hopes, and compassions is political in the extreme. To refuse cruelty—to refuse to participate in the machine of production and consumption that global capital both enables and requires for survival—is practically unpatriotic. One has to talk about politics when talking about Jane Cooper because her concerns are human—individual and human—and so wedded thus as a conscientious refusal of what might otherwise seem the inevitable advance of "civilization," which is anything but "civil."

In an early poem called "Letters" (57), Cooper presents an idea of the individual body fluidly woven into the fabric of time, the surrounding world, and the processes of aging and decay inherent in life. In the first section of the poem, she writes:

That quiet point of light
trembled and went out.

Iron touches a log:
it crumbles to coal, then ashes.

The log sleeps in its shape.
A new moon rises.

Darling, my white body
still bears your imprint.

When the log succumbs to its natural process—not burned here but rather "touched" by the iron—it does not disappear but "sleeps in its shape." The new moon rising is an image of presence-by-absence—a moon real and extant but completely invisible. The speaker herself at last appears as the body that appears in the final couplet—a body that is also the log, the ash that remained, also the moon in the sky, also the quiet point of light of the first line. These are all things in the world that disappear and even after their disappearance have a life by what remains of them.

The second half of the poem shifts both sonically and physically, from outside to inside:

Wind chewed at the screen,
rain clawed at the window.

Outside three crows
make their harsh, rainy scraping.

Autumn has come
in early July.

On the ground white petals:
my rain-soaked letters.

We're immediately, in the second section, in the world of humans: inside a house protected from the howling elements that both "chew" and "claw," the wind, the rain, the crows. It's an unseasonable climactic shift in this short poem about mortality and endings, bodies becoming not what they were, autumn arriving two months early. The "letters" on the ground are gorgeous—"white petals" and "rain-soaked" but also heavy with meaning—they are communiqués from the speaker, things dropped on the ground, what remain after life, but also letters as in elemental parts of the communication itself. A body does not disappear but unravels itself, sheds its meanings into the earth.

When I see Cooper's spare couplets, I remember her moving around the kitchen slowly, deliberately, warming the cups with hot water, placing objects on a tray: the cups, a sugar dish, a creamer. The body determines how one experiences the actual world and so must also impact poetic form and how it tries to transmit experience. Cooper's poetic lines build themselves across the page in couplets, first one line then the other—you have to hear the line and the space that surrounds it.

Cooper writes here a poem about death and the changing of the seasons and ends it with letters dropped on the ground, the tree's white petals—images of beauty and transmission, in short what you would normally think of as life itself. It would be a mistake though to think of her vision of death as purely optimistic or needlessly sentimental. In her early poem "The Weather of Six Mornings," she comments on the possibilities of communication and transference with a little bit of a starker tone:

Sunlight lies along my table
like abandoned pages.

I try to speak
of what is so hard for me

—this clutter of a life—
Puritanical signature!

(58)

But in each of the six short lyrics that make up the poem cycle, Cooper does not try for a "resolution" at all; rather, each poem, loosely arranged, arrives at a failing point—a place the poet stops pushing against the ineffable. In this way, the poems—not an "epic" at all, but a form of "serial lyric"—accumulate into a quieter, more resigned wisdom than "epiphany." The little creatures of the natural world here, "insects, / pine needles, birch leaves // make a ground bass of silence / that never quite dies."

As these leaves, creatures, needles on the ground—as the letters from the previous poem—create a silence, the speaker hovers in the face of it, wondering what is the appropriate response. Moments of anticipation govern the couplets of the following section:

Treetops are shuddering
in uneasy clusters

like rocking water
whirlpooled before a storm.

Words knock at my breast,
heave and struggle to get out.

A black-capped bird
pecks on, unafraid.

Yield then, yield
to the invading rustle of the rain!

(59)

Cooper's fear of expressing herself is contrasted with the unafraid
bird, but it is not purely oppositional—even the trees in the earlier
couplet are shown to shudder. It's interesting that the action of
yielding to the rain, an acceptance of the world's actions as superior
and more important than the human struggle to communicate, fin-
ishes the piece. It is not really a sublimation of the self to nature but
rather a release of the individual ego into the fact of larger exis-
tence. Against the Platonic ideal of man as measure of the universe,
Cooper situates herself not as an individual body/spirit responding
to a Creator, but rather as a constituent part of Creation.

Though Cooper yields to the rain here, in the following poem,
she finds that "a man's voice / refuses to be absorbed" (60). The
distance of her friend's death is incomprehensible and though the
friend's ashes "float out to sea," Cooper still hungers for "some
marker." We want to know that the human body, the individual
person, will still be remembered, still matters in some way. Burning
of a body to ashes and subsequent dispersal of those ashes is the
deepest form of metaphor for the soul's ultimate anxiety: that it is
mortal, that death is eternal, that the self is annihilated upon its
separation from carnate matter.

This anxiety plays out in seven lines of conditional clause in a
mere ten-line poem. "If the weather breaks / I can speak of your
dying," Cooper reasons, but after five more lines she says also, "I can
speak of your living," grammatically equating the two actions as the
same action (61).

Once again, Cooper does not come across as optimist. It's the
disappearing friend, the parting of the two that preoccupies her:

Now all the years in between
flutter away like lost poems.

And the morning light is so delicate,
so utterly empty. . . .

at high altitude, after long illness,
breathing in mote by mote a vanished world . . . .

The dissolution of the physical association of the two made by the friend's departure, the dispersal of the years into wind and light, the empty light, the subtlety and quietness with which these images are drawn all serve to create a tender emotional mood in the final line—"mote by mote a vanished world"—with the final ellipsis drifting into silence. Again, the white light is filtering through the curtain windows; Jane is putting the cup down into the saucer with the lightest clinking. I'm sitting back in the cushions, feeling unkempt, clumsy, too loud whenever I try to answer one of her questions. I sent her a few poems after that, and she wrote back to me several times. We tried a few times to meet again before she left New York City but didn't manage it. I would often guiltily swipe up any used copies of *The Flashboat* I could find—guiltily because I was denying other poetry-lovers the chance to find this book, but it is the one book I continued to give as gifts to anyone I needed to. I would have a stash of them on my bookshelf just to give away. When I couldn't explain poetry or why I write it to myself or anyone else, I had this book.

When I was working on final versions of my own poems for the publication of my first book *The Far Mosque*, I always held the last poem of the sequence "The Weather of Six Mornings" in my head. To be specific, it was the final three lines of the poem:

Rest.
A violin bow, a breeze

just touches the birches.
Cheep—a new flute

tunes up in a birch top.
A chipmunk's warning skirrs. . . .

Whose foot disturbs these twigs?
To the sea of received silence

why should I sign
my name?

(63)

11

What's resting in the line can be the poem itself, all creation, or that violin bow. A bow at rest on a string is preparing to make music or has just completed it—either way the music's silence resonates like the breeze, the baby bird in the tree, the chipmunk. After all the animal speech—a noisy poem after all—the presence of a human foot on twigs seems unbearable and unnecessary, leading to the stunning final question. What reason, then, Cooper asks, to add anything at all to silent sounds of creation?

But that stunning question of Cooper's—made more magnificent by its publication as the closing poem of her first collection—is not meant to be rhetorical but real. She does not leave it hanging in space but spends a career at the liminal edge of silence negotiating the relationship between an individual and corporeal existence and the fact of creation. The poetry may seem spiritual, but it is precisely the border between the tangible body and the ineffable nature of the spirit that Cooper seeks to know and understand.

Like many writers who came of age during World War II and its aftermath, Jane Cooper's first work engaged humans in a landscape of war. She comments on the relationship between beauty and experience: "I never could get over the peculiar beauty of a bombed out landscape," she writes of her experiences in Europe after the war, though conceding she only saw them "once the worst had been cleaned up, once the summer field flowers—poppies and fireweed and ragwort—had seeded themselves and started blooming over the rubble." She could not help but feel "guilt because I found the desolation visually beautiful."

Additionally, after writing an entire book of these poems—which would have been her first collection, a book she referred to as a "woman's experience of war"—she stopped writing and never tried to publish these poems. She engages the question of why she stopped writing in her long essay "Nothing Has Been Used in the Manufacture of This Poetry That Could Have Been Used in the Manufacture of Bread," which she reprinted in each of two books following her debut collection. She initially claims, as Grace Paley suggested, that "men's lives seemed more central than ours, almost more truthful" (101). It's true that Cooper most frequently positions herself in these political poems as a witness, an observer, someone who exists in the war only peripherally, not implicated. Only much later, in poems like "Clementene" and "Hotel de Dream," does Cooper explicitly confront her own complicity in oppression and the war that a position as bystander or witness to atrocity encompasses. In Cooper's case, it is her "sensuous, . . . / unjust white child's past" that she must come to terms with (190). In "Clementene," Cooper writes of her shock as a young girl when she learns that the seamstress who worked for her family had been passing for white. "Why, if I was not an accomplice," Cooper wonders, "did I feel—do I feel still—this complex shame?" (208).

Despite feelings of guilt from necessary implication in the forces of history—even these days, every one of us is contributing nearly 55 cents from every single one of our tax dollars to the U.S. military budget, the highest percentage of the overall national budget of any nation in the world—Cooper does, in the remarkable poem "The Flashboat" that takes place as a dream, describe the challenges of stepping out of the role of "witness" and into the role of actual participant.

In the dream, a ship is sinking, a bell is ringing, the ice around the ship is breaking apart. In this dire situation, one of the ship's officers—"my torturer who assumes we think alike"—is interrogating Cooper. "*Are you a political activist?*" he asks. To which she replies, "*No, I'm a teacher.*" It's the wrong answer—he confiscates her passport and locks it away. "Was I wrong to declare myself innocent?" she wonders (143).

At the end of the poem, the ship is sinking; the crew are making ready the lifeboats; and she is offered either a space on a larger, comfortable boat with the other women and the captain in charge or a position on the smaller "flashboat," which will require everyone to row, to lead the way to rescue. She writes, "For a moment, I hesitate, worrying about my defective blood," but then:

> . . . My voice with its crunch of bone
> wakes me: *I choose*
> *the flashboat!*
>> work,
>>> the starry waters

> (144)

That mention of a voice with a "crunch of bone" is wonderful and ominous, and it also signals the breaking of the poem from prose paragraphs to three verse lines at the end, the final two indented for added emphasis. Of particular subtle effect is the comma following the word "work," which changes its meaning from a verb into a more powerful and ongoing presence as a noun. The idea of "work," the rowing of the flashboat, is also equated with the starry waters themselves, making action of any kind not a transitive condition leading from a beginning to a desired result but rather a fixed quality of motion in the world, an eternity of breath, a body that exists, a universe that depends on inflow and outflow, perpetual "action."

Cooper does therefore "implicate" herself as a positive agent, whether she was a "bystander" or not during the war years.

In "Nothing Has Been Used in the Manufacture of This Poetry That Could Have Been Used in the Manufacture of Bread," she goes on to reveal the true reason she could not publish the earlier poems: she "couldn't face out the full range of intuition" the poems revealed. Even in her writing about war and bodies in a general sense, she was facing the more frightening subject of liminality between the life of the body and its death, the sounds of the world at peace and war, and their cessation. There is, after all, something truly horrifying about the silence at the end of bombing, the silence at the end of a storm, at the end of the bomb tests. "Why did I feel the need," she asks herself, "to write about the holocaust almost more than individual human relations, or to disguise my purpose to myself?" She goes on to realize, "In any case, by 1951 the war had begun to seem like a mask, something to write *through* in order to express a desolation that had become personal."

So when Cooper poses the question in 1969, "to the sea of received silence // why should I sign / my name?" she asks of herself a real question past this question, not just with a spiritual dimension referring to the problem of the human body within the matrix of creation, but another question with real material and political consequences: How can one write about the body as it exists in the world, remaining true to the individual life but conscious of the problematic dehumanization the twentieth century seemed to be engendering? Her answer to both of these questions simultaneously was a stunning series of poems written in the last two decades of her writing life, many of which, like her earlier poems, she withheld from publication until the 2000 release of *The Flashboat: Poems Collected and Reclaimed.*

Did the poems feel too personal, too hermetic? Did she see them as primarily building blocks representing hinge moments in her poetics from period to period? At any rate, they are charged with energy and space; dynamic and alarming, they now feel like essential documents anticipating in many ways the space-laden, fractured, yet intensely personal, lyrics of many younger poets writing today.

Cooper wrote her way out of her earlier more formal work. Large spaces began opening up in the poems, silences, not only literal but silences of energy, much the way large, flat color panes rise out of and interrupt the otherwise frenetic energy of Hoffmann's canvases. Her poem "Messages" answers back—in style, at least—to the delicate couplets of "The Weather of Six Mornings" or "Letters":

Ragged and thrashing
the road between me and the ocean—

I trip on stumps.
A gull flies over:

Guilt! guilt! your father is dying!
The woods are studded with poisonous berries.

(125)

The energy is very different here from the quiet and deliberate lines of the earlier poems. Lines are interrupted and the couplets themselves are split in action between the first line and the second line. As the speaker trips, the bird flies over but does not speak until the first line of next couplet. But the second line of that couplet does not complete the thought but rather moves on into the landscape. Besides the quick shifts in energy, the tripping both of sound and speaker, the poem introduces an idea of opposition, things that can be one thing or another:

a few stars telegraph:
Go back. Or else welcome.

(125)

These "Messages" are very different from the communiqués of "Letters," where the speaker felt herself dissolving into creation, participating in, dropping her letters down as leaves or petals fall, part of a natural dissolution. The speaker here is troubled, resistant, unsure how it is one is able to send her message—rather than delicate and rhapsodic couplets, a seamless communication, the later poet is anxious, frustrated, and finally communicates the only way she dares—in bits and pieces, not like a letter at all, but closer to the telegraph communication of the stars:

Approaching my life I am terrified.
Stars in the mud trip me up.

Terrified, I lug stone after stone
up the wide, foot-bruising ladder of night.

Stones in a ring can't define it:
Night.   Lake.   Mirror.   Deep.   Only

(125)

Needless to say—or perhaps one needs indeed to say it—the last line is a stunner, both in the context of Cooper's work and in the context of the poem itself. It is the breakdown of the sentence and possibility of meaning, but simultaneously a wholesale trust in language itself to make meaning. We travel into the atmosphere of the lake, word by word, deeper and deeper until the final word—a word of singularity, a word of doubt, ultimately a word of conclusion, but thank God for Jane Cooper's trust in the absolute energy of silence to forgo the final period, which if added, would have undone the whole motion of the poem. She is so much a master of sound that a single punctuation mark removed—or added where it does not belong as we saw in the final moment of "The Flashboat"—can sound volumes of resonance. She tries here in "Messages" to begin documenting her work of allowing the "received silence"—the silence of poetry, the silence after war, the silence of awe in the soul—into her body, her days, her noiseful life.

"Scattered Words for Emily Dickinson" and "S. Eliason 66"—both poems written in the 1970s but withheld from publication until 2000—are companion poems of sorts, each about the painting hanging in Cooper's apartment. The painting was done by Cooper's friend Shirley Eliason and depicts Dickinson and her friend Charles Wadsworth, one of the men speculated to be the recipient of her infamous "Master Letters."

"Scattered Words" unfolds in three short sections of lyric writing, narrative description, a list of "scattered words," and a piece of found text. It imitates (and prefigures in the next poem) Dickinson's desperate and powerful attachment to Wadsworth, one that, like all of Dickinson's attachments, remained somehow crucially or necessarily *detached* in the final account. The body of the poem squirms away from its subject, and the energy raised up has nowhere else to go but the next poem. At first glance, a reader would say a poem like this is a failure or maybe at most the first half of a poem which has no second half; but perhaps more honestly, it was thirty years ahead of its time—Cooper had to wait a little while for the light inside the text to be seen for what it was: a visionary explanation of the subject/body's tenuous relationship to the lyric. A poem that escapes poetry. Meaning it is still breathing on the page.

The poem's short first section reads:

Inside the crate, dark
as corn in its sheath   sheet lightning

(146)

The enjambment between lines and the lacuna in the second line, the wordplay across that space—"sheath sheet"—create an intimate and energetic space. One thinks the painting in its crate, radiating energy, is something of a stand-in for the figures themselves depicted there, their passion barely contained.

at the conservatory door   they
start forth

flashbulbs!

ochre   orange   flame   black   black   white

Their energy is purely transformed by the flashbulb of the painter's attention, scholars going through Dickinson's private letters and speculating about her most intimate relationships being like paparazzi of the present moving backwards in time. The moment of the flashbulbs is a hinge between the dynamism of the couple— again unfolding with unusual enjambment and lacuna—and the "scattered words" themselves. The energy here is not allowed to explode out, but rather from the chaotic chain of words, Cooper introduces found text from the exhibit catalogue:

Brilliant Pioneer Roots   and
difficult geography of the face of a friend:
(brilliant) notes from the painter's (my friend's) catalogue
(difficult) notes from the painter's (a pioneer's) catalogue

With the lovely parentheticals, Cooper allows the "brilliance" and "difficulty" to be both acknowledged and unsaid, to be "background" in the painting sense. She also imposes her personal connection to the work in the second parenthetical—in the first line linking herself with Eliason, in the second line crucially linking Eliason to Dickinson herself. She puts herself in the poem personally, the way Eliason finds herself inside Dickinson. This occupation of one body inside the other is exactly what was happening in the earlier poem "Messages"—the body of the poem inside the poem.

Oppositional philosophies of the body and spirit are either dualistic—saying the body is the mortal part and the spirit is immortal—or nondualistic—saying the body and the spirit are inherently wedded, one in the same being. Cooper, on the other hand, wrestles with the separation of writer of the poem and poem, painter and subject painted. These musings take us back to the initial lines of the first section, which have no immediate referent until the mention of the painting in the second numbered section. One is reminded of the poet herself inside the crate of her poem and also of Dickinson, declining to sign her first letter to Higginson, instead signing a small card which she sealed in a second smaller envelope to include with the unsigned letter. A body inside a body inside a body.

Then fabulously, what does the poem do with this fever of images, this back-and-forth set of readings in the first two sections? It moves into a completely unrelated scene in the third section:

> So the stolid-looking veteran
> (G.I. Bill, History of the Language)
> told me, speaking of combat:
> *In the least space*
> *between two bodies*
> *there is room*
> *for mystery*

(146)

She takes us completely away from the painting itself to another figure having a conversation with her about a different subject, so we are meant to travel some distance by applying his speech metaphorically to the painting we have heard described. His speech is not reported in a prose line but in poetic lines that freight the breaks with space and distance. "Space," "bodies," "room," and "mystery" allow the starkness of the painting, the moment it depicted, to fill us at the end of the poem.

It's the least space between two bodies that resonates the most—between Dickinson and Wadsworth, between the painting and its case, between Eliason and her work, between Cooper and the poem. It's a mystery the last line of the poem tells; it is "sheet lightning" the opening section says, but most of all, we end up remembering the veteran himself is not talking about painting or poetry but about combat and death.

Is it enough to delineate the tense moment between creator and creation, to point out that art cannot contain its subject at all or be contained by it, that even—as we know—Dickinson cannot yet approach Dickinson? Not for Jane Cooper. She proceeds past the moment of tension into the inevitable dissolution in the next poem, "S. Eliason 66." In this case, one of the dissolutions in a portrait is the death and disappearance of the subjects of the painting:

> She is just leaving the room.
> He fades to a china cup.
>
> (147)

Subjects having neatly departed the scene, the painter herself, the actual process of creating the painting, and the landscape in which the painting was created are all conflated into a brief and frenetic stanza. Once the reader is disoriented with this kaleidoscopic presentation, Dickinson and her life are reintroduced into the landscape, now occupying the same space as the painter's own mental processes:

> Velocity fraught with gold,
> with *menace of light,* atomic secrets—
> An aroused skin opens over the Great Plains.
> October leaves rain down.
>
> Corn in conflagration!
> The great retreats of the Civil War!
> Marriage in conflagration!
>
> (147)

What's funny is that I remember the painting in Cooper's apartment, but I cannot remember where it hung. You would think it a riot of color, the trembling figures within inches of each other, the space between two bodies unbearably close, but the strange part is that it's the space and not the figures I remember. They are at either end of the canvas, painted quite stiffly, she in "her Puritan white dress" and he "in his fiberboard suit." Between: that I remember. A field of luminous golden light, painted in swathes, smoothly, with white coming through. It's that immense space suspended that dominates the vision, crowds the figures themselves nearly out of the field of vision, echoes with all that was unsaid between the two, all that remains unsaid.

Perhaps the space also reflects the Iowa landscape in which Eliason was working, mirroring the private spaces in Dickinson's mind, the "desolation" of which Cooper spoke in her own life. The "Marriage in conflagration" suddenly seems very ominous, looming very large—not merely Wadsworth's marriage itself, but the very idea of "marriage"—of joining between objects and people. The space between the two friends seems to endanger any possibility of it.

Cooper has a vision of integration past all the space and danger it entails:

Years—an empty canvas.
She scrawls across radiant space

E . . . I . . . SON! *I made this.* The date.
Name within name.

The space then represents not only physical distance but time. One is tempted to misread "scrawl" as "crawl"—as the letters of Eliason's name are contained in Emily Dickinson's name, one word is contained in the other. There's suddenly then something comforting about being sheathed, being contained—to live within another person. Cooper celebrates Eliason's transference here—from alienation to enveloping within the work of art, within Dickinson herself. She accomplishes this by the act of traveling across the distance between artist and art, by claiming it. The glyph "E . . . I . . . SON"—the scrawl across radiant space—and the italic of the painter finally speaking for herself, signing and dating her work, all become powerful glyphs of reconciliation with the separated being—such reconciliation not being a dissolution of one body into another, but the housing rather of one body *within* the other, that word "within" in the final line resting comfortably between the "names" of the two women so important to Jane Cooper.

She is thus able to find in language itself the space and elasticity to begin exploring the sound and spirit inherent in writing, the vowels and the way they open up spaces in the body. The relationship between an individual and the community and world around her becomes then not a space of alienation but instead the space of possibility, the space of achieving the state of "within."

"Starting with a Line from Roethke," another of the withheld poems, demonstrates Cooper's far-ranging concern with sound and open spaces in the language. She moves in it from meditation to concrete observation, using the syllables themselves to create a wonderful music. The short twelve-line poem opens with four couplets that mirror each other:

> *To have the whole air!*
> To own, for the moment, nothing.
>
> The purl of a wood-thrush winding down through the blazing
>   afternoon.
> The least flick of leaves.
>
> Sunlight as energy
> but diffused until it becomes the soft clang of poems
>
> approaching from a great way off
> out of the cave of the past. . . .
>
> (150)

The vowels unfold into the air in the first couplet and echo into space in the fourth couplet here. Between them, couplets of uneven line lengths. See how the long line sets up a series of long vowel sounds and soft consonants, a wind through the natural world that turns on the second short line and that delicious "flick." The couplet after this reverses the strategy and introduces the unseen bell in the phrase "soft clang of poems." After the sound plays itself through the "cave of the past" and drifts away on the ellipse, Cooper closes the poem with a penultimate couplet of exciting and sensual music (Cooper pronounced the word "sexual" with a hard "k" sound followed by an "s" sound rather than the softer and more common "sh" sound—which is to say, the word "sexual" would have sonically called back to the "exuberant" of the previous line) and then a final couplet in which the still unnamed bell literally rings off across water. Not since Poe's "tintinnabulation" has a bell rung itself through language as finely as the "soft clang" of the unmentioned ocean buoy in the word "Tintagel" at the end of this poem:

> Frieda Kahlo's exuberant fruit,
> hacked open and sexual, or
>
> cliffs ringing with the calm off Tintagel.
> Calm off Tintagel.

(150)

The poem works sonically from the beginning, drawing the sounds inside itself until the final enactment of ringing. The text itself becomes a human body, breathing in and out, living in space, no subject really, other than itself.

One of the most precious things about Cooper's poetic body of work is that it really *is* a body. Not comprised of discrete books published one after the other punctuated by the occasional "new and selected" retrospective, Cooper's books instead accrete slowly, one after the other, each including work from the book before it, often revised subtly in pieces and places, three of her five books also including the prose essay we discussed earlier.

Her poem "Waiting" is included in three of her five books, *Maps & Windows, Scaffolding,* and *The Flashboat,* in three different versions.

The poem begins, in all three versions:

> My body knows it will never bear children.
> What can I say to my body now,
> this used violin?
> Every night it cries out strenuously
> from its secret cave.

(140)

The body is at once extremely personal and utterly objectified—an object, even if a beautiful instrument, separate from the spirit's identity nonetheless. She goes on:

> Old body, old friend,
> why are you so unforgiving?
>
> Why are you so stiff and resistant
> clenched around empty space?
> An instrument is not a box.

But suppose you are an empty box?
Suppose you are like that famous wooden music hall in Troy, New York,
waiting to be torn down
where the orchestras love to play?

She allows herself the ultimate question, the one the soul with all of its attendant anxieties about mortality and permanent cessation with the body's death never even allows itself to ask, the question a childless woman (or man!) approaching old age might wish to avoid: "But suppose you are an empty box . . . waiting to be torn down. . . ." Though in the first version of the poem, the body cries out "desolately," in the later versions of the poem, the body cries out "strenuously." Once more, she asserts the sublimation of the human individual to the larger force of creation.

The first version of "Waiting," published in *Maps & Windows* in 1974, ends with the couplet:

Let compassion breathe in and out of you
filling you with poems[1]

But by 1984's *Scaffolding,* Cooper opts for something a little more essential, a little closer to the source of poetry than the actual word "poems," and closes the poem like this:

Let compassion breathe in and out of you
filling you, singing[2]

But when Cooper revises all of her earlier work, restoring many previously unpublished poems in *The Flashboat: Poems Collected and Reclaimed,* she revisits "Waiting" once again. This time, instead of seeing "singing" as the reification of "poems," she sees the whole motion of breath as a process, an action unto itself that doesn't end, as in "work, the starry waters" in the poem "The Flashboat." Instead of a mere receptacle being filled, the body itself becomes the instrument of compassion—she ends the poem like this:

Let compassion breathe in and out of you,
breathe in and out of you

(140)

23

Notes

1. Jane Cooper, *Maps & Windows* (New York: Macmillan, 1974), 27.
2. Jane Cooper, *Scaffolding* (London: Anvil Press Poetry, 1984), 90.

STEPHEN TAPSCOTT

"Mercator's World"
Jane Cooper's Early Work

Early work often anticipates and so helps to define the writer in her prime. My favorite example of this effect is Jane Cooper's early poems, which were intended to be a book but, in fact, were never published as such. Years later, however, Cooper did publish fifteen of them as the opening section of her second published collection, identifying them (under the title "Mercator's World") as earlier and, in an essay also included in the volume, theorizing the reasons for their belatedness.

In the essay, Cooper holds the phenomenon up to the clarifying light of her lucid emotional intelligence, reclaiming and reframing those poems, reconnecting to the energies of the earlier writer-self. That process feels to me like a metonymy of what I revere about Jane Cooper's later poems and the arc of her career: the factual experience is not *so* extraordinary—it's a life like another life—but the clarifying moral/emotional intelligence with which Cooper renders that experience changes it.

"Mercator's World" is a factual world—a portrait of a world more than of a person in that world, as the title suggests—of measurement and social-norms, and of a narrator's efforts to adapt to new fixed formulations and the traumas of World War II. It also includes her struggles to reconcile a desire for peacetime stability with traumatic memory *and* with the desire to write, a desire that seems to resist normalization. "Why, while cities burn, do I still live? . . . I have no faith, I do not expect to recover / Any but myself, the unit, man." The poems advert to other struggles, other people's suffering, a sense of belatedness—part survivor-guilt, part aspiration. The "urge to tell the truth," in one poem, "strips sensuality" from an encounter (84). The imagination of a former prisoner of war locks him in "his bell of glass / Which keeps even the girls he kisses from touching his face" (80). The connecting thread—as Cooper understood it in 1951—would dramatize this belatedness, in "a

25

book of war poems from a woman's point of view." Perhaps, she speculates in 1974, this second-order relation to experience is what caused her to set the book aside; she alludes to Grace Paley's suggestion that one problem for female writers was that women's experience wasn't acknowledged *as* experience. ("The men's lives seemed more central than ours, almost more truthful. They had been shot down, or squirmed up the beaches. We had waited for their letters" [101].) "To be a man" was to be "the crowd's hero."

I think these early poems do displace the experience of the observer, in poems of the home-front war continued in peacetime but with discordant subtexts. Repeatedly, women's experience is ironized. A speaker (Maud Gonne in old age?) recalls being idealized but forgotten if an actual poem distracted the male Poet/Lover, and from such deflections she learned her own fierce life skills. ("I still remember evenings when I learned // The tricks of style." ["Long View from the Suburbs," 87]). In "In a Room with Picassos," an artist's model defies him to understand what her actual experience is. She resists, that is, becoming "a Picasso" ("Draw as you will there are no images / Which exactly reproduce this state of mind . . ." [90]). In a Hardy-like sonnet, Eve faces the challenges of post-war American women ("time has come / When she shall be delivered . . . / Marriage must take her now"), though her restricted choices sound as if the social-conditions of mid-century America were essential conditions of women's lives (78). These poems—their war-trauma and bomb-blasts—frame these political dynamics largely as gendered experience but also work against gender constrictions.

Or begin to work, since, in retrospect, we want the subtexts to be declaring resistances that the poems don't explore. The image of Mercator-lines appears directly in "For a Boy Born in Wartime":

Head first, face down, into Mercator's world
Like an ungainly rocket the child comes
. . . .
Inheritor of our geographies,
Just as we rise to slap your fluttering cry. . . .

(79)

The figure—a body as a kind of falling bomb—is a familiar war-image—Yeats's in "An Irish Airman Foresees His Death," Jarrell's in

"Death of a Ball-Turret Gunner"—but Cooper turns it into the birth of a child falling into a chartered world; she wonders about the child's future in that world. The poem anticipates Plath's "Morning Song," with the child's arrival making the speaker realize something of the nature of the parental world where the child arrives.

As she abandoned the early poems, Cooper explored in her journal some reasons that the project felt problematic—concerning slippage between the rhetoric of action ("war poems") and postwar conditions of different kinds of "conflict":

> Now I can no longer capture those moods . . . and so the whole rhetorical machinery seems . . . out of date. My poetry was heroic poetry, and now what I have to say doesn't concern heroes. . . .
>
> (120)

And yet these journal-accounts of slowly talking herself out of the war-poem project don't seem the complete truth. "Guilt, war, disease—pillars of violence / To keep a roof of symbols over my head." Closer to the bone, it seems to me, is the journal's recognition that the issue is not rhetoric, but authenticity:

> In any case, by 1951 the war had begun to seem like a mask, something to write *through* in order to express a desolation that had become personal. . . .
>
> (112–13)

The essay explaining Cooper's decision to abandon the early poems seems haunted by parallel questions that other writers—Tillie Olsen in *Silences*, Adrienne Rich in *On Lies, Secrets, and Silence*—were pursuing: issues of women writers and social expectations, marriage/children, demands of professionalism and the private life. Cooper speculates that although she never married, she also suffered a crippling silence, an internalization of those forces that externally might have affected a woman who chose marriage. Does the broken promise of the first book resemble the silence enforced on other women? she implicitly asks. Does the female writer—do I—internalize these powers so that we work against ourselves while not explicitly recognizing it?

The essay suggests that something like that *is* happening in the poems of Jane Cooper's unpublished first book. I think I understand why the younger writer would leave these poems and refocus, even stop writing for a while. The book that "replaced" the Mercator poems as Cooper's first book was *The Weather of Six Mornings*, a more conventionally serene, mature work. Less formally conventional and yet less tonally fierce, the poems anticipate her later style; the emotional arc of the poems moves repeatedly toward acceptance, reconciliation. *No more elegies!* one poem exclaims (68). The last concludes with "an air of departure [. . .] / Leaving behind a breath of love and angers" (71).

Metaphors of seeing inform the Mercator poems; compounded with war-memories, they become images of radioactive "looking"—in x-rays, in bodies after a bomb-blast. *Weather* speaks through a self looking through a window, not through a wall or another's body. This accepting attitude, a selfhood larger than the single self, permits the *Weather* poems finally to address the griefs the post-war Mercator poems had attempted, "war poems from a woman's point of view." Here is "The Faithful," from a decade later:

Once you said joking slyly, *if I'm killed*
I'll come to haunt your solemn bed,
I'll stand and glower at the head
And see if my place is empty still, or filled.

What was it woke me in the early darkness
Before the first bird's twittering?
—A shape dissolving and flittering
Unsteady as a flame in a drafty house.

It seemed a concentration of the dark burning
By the bedpost at my right hand
While to my left that no man's land
Of sheet stretched palely as a false morning. . . .

All day I have been sick and restless. This evening
Curtained, with all the lights on,
I start up—only to sit down.
Why should I grieve after ten years of grieving?

What if last night I was the one who lay dead?
While the dead burned beside me
Trembling with passionate pity
At my blameless life and shaking its flamelike head?

(28)

This poem reverses a Thomas Hardy-like ghost-moment: where Hardy would track the compensatory, guilt-inflicting appearance of a spirit after a life of failed hope, Cooper locates the disappointment in the survivor's "guiltless" loyalty, her voluntary refusal of subsequent experience. The first stanza recalls a conversation between separating lovers; in italics, a serviceman about to be posted somewhere dangerous teases his lover about conventional fidelity, though the stanza closes ambiguously. We assume he is hoping that if he is killed, his place in her "solemn bed" will not be "filled" by someone else—the sly-joking, affectionate (if somewhat controlling) convention. (And the conventional form—the pattern of full rhymes, in a strict abba rhyme scheme—reinforces this sense of steady Mercator-lined conventionality, even an enclosing entrapment.) The poem reverses the convention, heart-wrenchingly. A ghost might appear—if so, we sense, he'd be disappointed by the continued "fidelity" of the woman after a decade of grief, the no-name's-land of sheet stretching pale on her bed signifying a waste of vitality. Her nonparticipatory, blameless life "has been a kind of not living"—a deflection or evasion of the real difficulty of living with tragic knowledge. Or there simply may be no ghost—an equally wistful possibility, which would make her chaste "fidelity" an even greater irony, her restlessness signaling her own knowledge of the waste.

I read this poem also as a synecdoche for the "war poems from a woman's point of view." I think it no coincidence that it took a silence of five years, and a total of a decade's time, for this poem—the survivor's grief and then the self-consciousness about that grief—to be written. That time-lag suggests something about the nature of the first-book project, about Cooper's need to leave it, and about what it means—or meant in 1969/1974—to return to that earlier project and that earlier self. It strikes me as no coincidence that that poem—dramatizing the passive guilt of the observant citizen witness—is realized during America's war in Vietnam and that period's turmoil of conscience for those on the home front. Cooper's reclaiming that first-book energy—declaring not only a new point-of-origin for her career as a whole, but the self-conscious *process* of reclaiming those early ("political") poems and of recognizing, retrospectively, what other energies had been at work in them—strikes me as a model of a movement-of-mind throughout her career. Often, she recognizes that she'd had the experience but missed the meaning (until later), discovering that feelings or ideologies she'd thought had structured a moment or a period of her life were different from what she'd thought: more complex, more political, more power-inflected.

The Mercator poems have an element of dismayed rage, of self-accusation, that can't quite surface for articulation until later. I think their rectilinear expectations (Mercator map-lines represent the center of the field well but distort peripheries) are so internalized that they're unsustainable as statements about external politics. It's too simple to say that the elements of war-witness that had been the discourse of the earlier project got displaced into troubled personal/love/relationship poems. Of course, that displacement does happen (that POW's defensiveness continues through post-war love-relationships), but by the early 1970s, Cooper could articulate self-mistrust, even anger at the self, for complicity in one's difficulties. That's the great discovery of "The Faithful": despite the wrenching recognition that she's squandered vitality in the service of grief, there's an element of belated judgment against the self, an acknowledgement of how one has conspired against one's self, for reasons that seemed socially prescribed at the time. Cooper remained loyal to a grief past its due-date: she's learning such loyalty can become a mask or deflection of the pain of experiencing grief-through-time. She's conspired against herself, slowly failing to reclaim her own agency. This poem of loyalty to older responsibilities is the last of the "war" poems, and it anticipates a thematic in Cooper's later work, by which responsible loyalty to older forms of the self can be restrictive. The poem claims a new female-consciousness of holding-oneself-to-account. I admire how the tone sustains the dismayed anger of the earlier poems while repositioning the slightly too-eager reconciliations of *Weather*. (I think this eventually was one of Sylvia Plath's great discoveries, too; the narrator of "Daddy" is as angry at herself as she is at either parent.)

One great discovery in Cooper's later poems is the serene joy of patient responsible self-knowledge. In this sense, her reframing the narrative, retrospectively examining her reasons for abandoning her first book, are fresh and helpful. Reclaiming part of the abandoned book and reorganizing those energies into *Maps & Windows* and later work, Cooper reintroduces the framework of "political" conscience but shifts the politics. Like the medieval "master-work," she highlights what had been there *in potentia* but moves—from the early politics of post-World War II (the sense-of-powerlessness of the citizen-observer) to the later politics of gender, enacting what Stevens called "the morality of the right sensation." I admire both the Mercator poems and *The Weather*, and I learn a lot from Jane Cooper's reasons for *not* publishing—for waiting to publish—the earlier series. In her calm responsible attentions, she turns constrictive Mercator map-lines literally into *Maps & Windows*.

JAMES WRIGHT

Review of *The Weather of Six Mornings*

As I read and re-read the achingly beautiful poems of Jane Cooper, winner of this year's Lamont Poetry Award, I begin to glimpse something of the relation between tradition and inspiration.

A helpful text comes from Santayana's *The Idea of Christ in the Gospels.* In the chapter "Inspiration," the philosopher remarks as follows:

> The most skeptical philosopher when dreaming believes in his dream. Its transformulations do not surprise him and its contradictions seem to him each a new revelation of the truth. He can begin to doubt only when some firm system of old inspirations crops up under his feet, and he feels the ground on which he is standing while his head is in the clouds. Such a system must first be built into the structure of language and buttressed by applications in the useful arts. Then, in contrast to these conventions by which mankind manages to live, new and bolder inspirations may seem disruptive and fantastic. There ensues a battle of inspirations, the new against the old, the native against the foreign, the more speculative against the more practical. But in themselves all inspirations are speculative: that which is practical and useful can be only the action that may accompany them.

If all inspirations are speculative, then the traditional is at least as open as the random. I realize that at least 750,000 of my readers are geniuses, who know, without giving thought, that poetry is a gift from God. But it is also a craft, and you do not learn how to manage it in an afternoon's random typing, comrades. Sir Thomas Wyatt wrote poems that are at once perfectly traditional and inescapably passionate. That is not bad for a fellow who is only 466 years old, give or take an eternity or two.

Jane Cooper's poetry belongs to Wyatt's tradition. Her mastery of the craft is such that the tone which her poems can convey is the tone of happiness. One example must serve. It is called "The Faithful."

Once you said joking slyly, "If I'm killed
I'll come to haunt your solemn bed,
I'll stand and glower at the head
And see if my place is empty still, or filled."

What was it woke me in the early darkness
Before the first bird's twittering?
—A shape dissolving and flittering
Unsteady as a flame in a drafty house.

It seemed a concentration of dark burning
By the bedpost at my right hand,
While to my left that no-man's land
Of sheet stretched palely as a false morning. . . .

All day I have been sick and restless. This evening
Curtained, with all the lights on,
I start up—only to sit down.
Why should I grieve after ten years of grieving?

What if last night I was the one who lay dead,
While the dead burned beside me
Trembling with passionate pity
At my blameless life and shaking its flamelike head?

The happiness which this poem conveys is the direct conse-
quence of the poet's mastery of her craft. To master a craft does not
mean that some clever person has figured out yet another cute way
to con the public by playing tricks with words instead of soup cans.
The mastery of craft means the mastery of emotion. In Miss Coo-
per's poems, the emotions are frequently almost unbearable: lone-
someness, ruefulness, and loss. The resonance of her poems arises
between the truth of her emotions and her technical mastery.

By one of those happy chances of human life, Thomas Hardy sat
down one afternoon during his eighty-eighth year and wrote a
poem called "Nobody Comes." On the same day, Miss Jane Cooper
was born. I believe that Thomas Hardy would have admitted that he
was wrong. I also believe that very great man would have been al-
most as happy at the arrival of Miss Cooper and her book as I am.
In the lovely lines of the young Mr. Kingsley Amis:

Women are really much nicer than men.
No wonder we like them.

NED BALBO

The Weather of Six Mornings
Deference and Defiance in Jane Cooper's Debut

By January 1969, when Macmillan published *The Weather of Six Mornings* as the Lamont Poetry Selection, Jane Cooper's poems had already graced the pages of *The New Yorker* and *Harper's Magazine* and won her several honors, including a Guggenheim fellowship and stays at Yaddo and MacDowell. The yellowed card slipped into my used first edition reminds me that the panel of judges consisted of Hayden Carruth, Donald Hall, Donald Justice, William Stafford, and James Wright—leading lights of the era's male-centric literary establishment—and that the contest was "established 'for the discovery and encouragement of new poetic genius.'" The author, born in 1924 but making her debut in middle age, might have smiled at that. After years of second-guessing whether the poems she wrote were ready, including a period in the 1950s when she gave up writing poetry, Jane Cooper was finally on her way.

Not everyone understood what she was after. The first edition's jacket flap promises poems "entirely her own—evocative, disciplined, filled with an authenticity and an authority which spring from deep personal experience" but adds that Cooper's "seemingly quiet poems juxtapose the world of physical reality and the world of dreams, so that both are equally imaginary, equally real." Less charitably, *Kirkus Reviews* called it a "collection of brief, watery poems, raising somnolent retrospective scenes and moods." The verdict: it was "tentative, diluted" and its author "as yet an unfocused talent." In their reliance on liminal states and spaces as metaphors for Cooper's poetry, the jacket copy's anonymous author and *Kirkus Review's* anonymous critic show much in common—and both miss the point.

In her 1974 essay "Nothing Has Been Used in the Manufacture of This Poetry That Could Have Been Used in the Manufacture of Bread," Cooper reflects on her first book's virtues and limitations. *The Weather of Six Mornings* was written mostly in her thirties, she writes:

And it's true that book is full of acceptances, even pieties, and not just formal ones. Above all, the self is seen as no more important than anyone else, a self in a world of selves who give one another strength and life.

In an era that celebrated Confessional poets like Robert Lowell and John Berryman (Cooper's former teachers at the Iowa Writers' Workshop) or women poets like Anne Sexton who specialized in self-disclosure, Cooper's more restrained approach—a poetic self attuned to a broader community and shared experience—seemed quaint. In 1947, while attending the first Oxford University summer school, her principle influences were Dylan Thomas, Gerard Manley Hopkins, and Yeats, she recounts, adding, "I'd long been familiar with the work of Auden and also Spender, and when I thought of a contemporary, politically aware tone of voice, that was the tone I still thought in." These influences (especially Auden's) shaped *The Weather of Six Mornings*, though Cooper had already begun to transcend this legacy's limitations.

Except for Muriel Rukeyser (who, to Cooper, seemed to be leading "a life of extraordinary courage") and Emily Dickinson (whose originality would become evident to Cooper only later)· there were "no women models as we now understand that word. I didn't even know many older women who worked." Noting that "men's praise of women poets didn't seem to go much beyond Marianne Moore and Elizabeth Bishop," at a time when women's poems "were still only sparsely represented in contemporary poetry anthologies," Cooper observes,

> Somehow I had absorbed out of the New Critical air itself . . . that women have trouble managing traditional meters with authority and verve and also can't handle long lines. . . . So I went to school to what models I could find—mostly the British poets already mentioned—to learn long rhythmic periods and metrical invention within the forms. The subjects I was writing about—war and relations between women and men—seemed also mostly to have remained the property of men.
>
> (109–110)

Still, despite her own youthful doubts or retrospective self-criticism, Cooper's metrical work is excellent. *The Weather of Six Mornings'* second and third sections consist largely of rhymed or slant-rhymed metrical poems; most feature a clear setting, strong core images, and a distinctive voice. Some recall the early verse of others who'd thrown off Auden's influence—Adrienne Rich, W. S. Merwin, or James Wright—so Cooper's own break with meter was nothing unusual. Though she'd later condemn a "perfectionism" she had to move beyond, the poems she produced are beautifully realized and technically accomplished.

They show variety, too. "Practicing for Death" is a coming-of-age poem whose child protagonist, immersed in catching butter-flies, is less aware of mortality's shadow than the poet looking back, yet Cooper's stanzaic and syntactic skill combine to memorable effect. In seven-line rhymed stanzas that feature pentameter and trimeter lines, she writes with admirable precision:

> Or I would watch you trembling on a branch
> Open and close with pure control your wings
> As if a steady hand
> Slowly could wind, unwind
> The coil that steeled those frail yet tensile springs,
> As if unhurried breathings
> Had drifted you aloft out of my reach.[1]

The end-rhymes are admirably unforced; the internal slant-rhymes (coil/steeled/frail/tensile) reinforce the sonic texture; and the image that emerges—the butterfly, "trembling," a tiny toy-like mechanism at rest or in weightless flight—is both apt and perfectly paced. Notable, too, here and elsewhere, is Cooper's success in long lines: clearly, the stereotype she'd absorbed had held no lasting power.

The best poems in *The Weather of Six Mornings* address relationships directly; "The Faithful," which Cooper called "the most truthful poem I was to write about World War II," and "Obligations," which she called "the most most satisfying challenge" of the poems she wrote in 1950–1951," are among them.

The speaker in "The Faithful,"[2] in dialogue with her beloved dead, recalls his joking threat to "haunt" her bed if he's "killed" to find out whether his place "is empty still, or filled." Though the speaker takes no lovers, years later she's "sick and restless," wondering, "Why should I grieve after ten years of grieving?" The closure relies on reversal: suppose the chastely faithful speaker is the one who's dead, trapped numbly in a kind of avoidance—avoidance of experience, avoidance of joy? Cooper's initially regular quatrains—an *abba* rhyme scheme, with the first and fourth lines in pentameter, the second and third in tetrameter—relax metrically as the poem proceeds, and its urgent voice—"What if last night I was the one who lay dead . . . ?"—is alert and acute, not somnolent.

Cooper called "Obligations"[3] an "honest poem, about an accepted human encounter, with its own built-in griefs." Three octaves in iambic pentameter are rhymed or slant-rhymed irregularly; the lovers' "clasp . . . is all the safety either of [them] hopes for." But *are* they safe, even at rest? Mortality, sharpened by war, encroaches, and realization beckons:

> What can your eyes lay claim to? What extreme
> Unction after love is forced upon us?
> The sun is setting now after its fullness
> While on the horizon like a fiery dream
> Wakes the long war, and shared reality,
> And death and all we came here to evade.

Here, Catholic ritual's final anointing is replaced by war's "reality"—one "shared" by all, not just the lovers who "evade" it only briefly.

Others poems addressing relationships include "To a Very Old Man, on the Death of His Wife," "Song: Staten Island Ferry," "3 : The Racetrack" (from the "Blue Spaces" sequence), and "In the Last Few Moments Came the Old German Cleaning Woman." The latter is especially compelling. Composed in rhymed sestets of loose tetrameter, the poem employs a final morning's "senseless chores / —Coffee and eggs and newspapers—" to explore imminent departure and lasting separation. Never again will the lovers meet here (or anywhere) for their liaisons; established routine will not "fix by ritual / the marriage [they] will never share."[4]

The death of Cooper's mother also provides essential subject matter. "For My Mother in Her First Illness, from a Window Overlooking Notre Dame"[5] opens by interrogating memory's failures—"Why can I never when I think about it / See your face tender under the tasseled light / Above a book held in your stubby fingers?"—and concludes, darkly, "How can I tell which one of us is absent?" In "The Faithful," Cooper asked the similar question, "What if last night I was the one who lay dead," preoccupied there, too, with a reversal of perspective (i.e., do the dead miss the living as the living miss the dead?): her means of exploring the grief exacted by loss. In "For My Mother . . . ," Cooper's six-line stanzas (in varying rhyme schemes and loose four- or five-beat lines) affectionately "reconstruct . . . feature by feature" the beloved parent: her "sailor's gaze, a visionary blue," a woman "[a]rrogant as a cathedral or the sea" with "ribs of quicksand feeling in [her] face." The portrait holds all the more impact for its final line, offered by a speaker "[a]lone and sick, lying in a foreign house."

"My Young Mother,"[6] a fine miniature, also echoes "The Faithful." Here, three free-verse quatrains capture the dream visitation of the title character: though middle-aged, the daughter-speaker, from "a corner of [her] dream," sees her mother standing near in a 1920s-style hat. Her identifying mole and disquieting expression—"as if I had nothing to give her—/ Eyes blue—brim dark—" call to the speaker "from sleep after decades," and there the poem ends. Its simplicity is haunting—literally.

The free verse tercets of "In the House of the Dying"[7] point toward Cooper's poetic future. "[T]ired aunts / whisper together under the kitchen globe," but this daughter-speaker, keenly aware of coming grief, feels cut off: "I am not one of them." Small but telling gestures define the poem: the speaker washing her hands "in a sheath of light," passages up and down the stairs to visit the dying mother. Though Cooper's use of meter and rhyme in other poems is exemplary, her move into free verse here opens up new possibilities: she is able to articulate her preoccupations—her personal quest—in plainer language.

> While the birth of love is so terrible to me
> I feel unworthy of the commonest marriage.
> Upstairs she lies, washed through by the two miracles.

The daughter-speaker sees herself as free of conventional ties but, for that reason, as someone who's failed "at birth and death"— unlike the dying mother able to dream of those "autumn nights when her children were born." "I've never married, have no children, so you could say my case was always different," Cooper states in her crucial essay. As an artist, Cooper is a woman apart from other women, but she is also connected to the larger community of creative women faced with the constraints and challenges of a broader masculine culture (including literary culture). Her feelings of self-doubt, of being "unworthy," are part of what silenced her in early days, while both kinds of birth—the "birth of love" and actual birth—provoke ambivalence: they are "the two miracles" that elude the daughter-poet even as she seeks survival as an artist.

The Weather of Six Mornings is framed by two sequences: "March" and the title sequence which ends the book. The latter[8] offers a moving summation of her themes. Each of six numbered sections contains five free-verse stanzas; the poem's central concern is how to speak of grief. In quiet lines suffused with each morning's natural imagery, "[w]ords knock at [the speaker's] breast, / heave and struggle to get out." A man is dead, and his cremated ashes "float out to sea," the poet addressing him directly: "If the weather breaks / I can speak of your dying, // if the weather breaks . . . I can speak of your living, // the lightning-flash of meeting. . . ." In a sequence whose concision heightens its power, Cooper knows just when to shift between voice and description: "Now all the years in between / flutter away like lost poems. // And the morning light is so delicate, / so utterly empty." Finally, she asks, "To the sea of received silence // why should I sign my name?" Will ending the sequence purge her of grief, and does she even *want* that purging? Or can she leave the poem in suspension, with memory—and grief—preserved? Further, in light of how silence claims us all, what is the value of writing poems—of authorship itself? Why bother to sign the name that's certain to vanish? "The Weather of Six Mornings" shows Cooper at her best, a master of subtle tonal shifts and narrative concision.

The sequence "March"[9] is less successful. In the foreword to *Scaffolding*, 1984's new and selected volume, Cooper writes, "In 1967, anguished by United States involvement in the Viet Nam war, I opened 'March' with images from other unjust wars."[10] The spare, free-verse poems of "March" are indeed powerful, with striking images of haiku-like simplicity, yet Cooper's foregrounding of voice and resonant detail at times sacrifices accessibility. "Feathers" opens the sequence: "I've died, but you are still living"—a line, according to Cooper's note, borrowed from Pasternak's *Doctor Zhivago*. In *Maps and & Windows,* the line is *not* italicized—contradictory when an "I" very much alive shows up. (Italics solve the problem in later collections.) In all versions, the speaker offers, "If I look down from my window / I can see one of the walks we used to take together," noting signs of an army's recent passage ("slight corpses, abandoned weapons"). But the poem's original closure is confusing: "As long as I do not go there / nothing can stop the huzzah of the male wind!" In both *Scaffolding* and *The Flashboat: Poems Collected and Reclaimed*, the penultimate line becomes, "Against the glass here, listen," which eliminates vagueness and reminds us that the speaker is looking through a window. The changed context sharpens the final line's wintry, war-torn setting and connects to the poet's body of work: "nothing can stop the huzzah of the male wind!" We hear Cooper's characteristic mix of deference and defiance: the "huzzah of the male wind"—the winds of war? Poetry's all-too-masculine weather?—will not be stopped: not yet.

Not every revision to "March" is significant, though sometimes it's surprising to see what Cooper leaves untouched. "Return" ("Back" in *Scaffolding* and *The Flashboat*) is an example. By referencing Henry Purcell's opera *Dido and Aeneas*, in which Carthage's queen is abandoned by the Trojan hero, the poem further explores the subject of women's grief in a soldier's absence. Cooper's intent is to blur the boundary between the opera's characters and the solitary listener-speaker, but the shift isn't entirely successful when a "you"—the absent lover, the speaker herself, Dido or Aeneas?—is addressed as if present: "Again, your eyes star / with salt as I choose my elegy"—an otherwise beautiful closure. By contrast, "No More Elegies," a strong poem in all versions, is revised repeatedly. The five-stanza poem of *The Weather of Six Mornings* loses its two opening stanzas in *Scaffolding*'s version; *The Flashboat* restores the original second stanza but not the original first stanza. That lost first stanza, a vivid seasonal evocation, reads:

Today the snow crunches underfoot
and squeaks dryly like compressed sugar.
Up the road run tire ribbons,
along the paths the quick prints of rabbits.

"No More Elegies" contrasts a frigid winter townscape under bright sun with the wish for early spring, as the speaker interprets overheard birdsong as "No more elegies!" The poet responds, "Poor / fools, they don't know it's not spring!": more of winter's losses are on the way. Of course, the question of what to cut or keep in any poem is difficult; still, Cooper's restlessness is interesting: both *Scaffolding* and *The Flashboat* shift the "March" sequence to *after* the rest of *Weather*. It's a smart move. The eight poems that comprise "March," written in 1967, are transitional, free of metrical constraints, and subtly voiced but sometimes cryptic. Individually arresting—"Middle Age" and "Smoke" ("Coda: Smoke" in *Scaffolding*, "Coda" in *Flashboat*) are especially strong; they gain resonance in the company of more accessible early poems.

As I hold my first edition of *The Weather of Six Mornings*, inscribed by Cooper in 1970 to poet-aviatrix Ann Darr, I think of time's long reach and the quiet power of these poems—poems less bound by gravity than their author herself believed. In 1974, when *Maps & Windows* appeared, *Kirkus Reviews* revised its estimation of the author: Cooper is "a poet of greater possibilities than her last book . . . suggests." When *Scaffolding* appeared, Wendy Salinger's generally even-handed commentary in *Iowa Review* looks for moments when "the soul will sing through the husk, the stripped-down life become a scaffolding for the spirit," but is largely disappointed. Is she is seeking the wrong rewards from Cooper's body of work? Salinger writes:

> [T]he language of these poems is almost, to borrow a phrase from one of them, "picked clean." There are poets—like Hopkins, Roethke—in whom the Spirit shakes loose a torrent of words. This is not the case with Jane Cooper. Her poetry, understated and unadorned by nature, becomes more so in reaching toward the transcendent. . . . [T]he poems ask more of the silences around them, the white spaces, than they deliver in words.

I would argue that Cooper's awareness of the interplay between spare language and the silence around it is one of her great virtues. By wrapping *The Weather of Six Mornings* in two of her sparest sequences, the first of them flawed though powerful, Cooper sought to remove the focus from older poems and her largely metrical apprenticeship; yet, it is the presence of these poems that clarifies the emotional tumult and reticent sensibility that define the title sequence, and they comprise a lively, varied collection in their own right. A poetry of understatement and concision always requires more of the reader than showier work, and time is kind to it, as the growth of Elizabeth Bishop's reputation has demonstrated. Cooper's poems are curt but bracing: most contain a note of elegy. Had Cooper continued to write in meter, there's every reason to believe she would likely have found ways to loosen her voice within its strictures. However, "Nothing Has Been Used . . ." closed the door on that alternative:

> . . . I can't be sorry that *The Weather of Six Mornings*, when it finally appeared, was based on certain rather broad human acceptances. I had to get through the perfectionism of those early poems, to learn that no choice is absolute and no structure can

save us. . . . All the more reason, I think, to accept as part of whatever I am now that young, cabined, often arrogant, but questing and vivid self whose banishment I've come to recognize as one more mistaken absolute.

(122)

We, too, must be grateful that Cooper's debut volume preserves that "vivid self" for us.

Notes

1. Jane Cooper, *The Weather of Six Mornings* (New York: Macmillan, 1969), 36.
2. Ibid., 17.
3. Ibid., 15.
4. Ibid., 43.
5. Ibid., 18–19.
6. Ibid., 47.
7. Ibid., 46.
8. Ibid., 48–51
9. Ibid., 3–10.
10. Jane Cooper, *Scaffolding: New and Selected Poems* (London: Anvil Press Poetry, 1984), vii.

JAN HELLER LEVI

"Ablaze, Scared Child!"

PRACTICING FOR DEATH

I

Monarch and fritillary, swallowtail—
Great butterflies red-brown or glossy black,
Spotted or striped or plain,
Each glistening with down—
I chased you through my earliest fields and back
Along a tangled track
To where the woods grew secret, dark and tall.

There you would disappear with a last hover,
Scurry or zigzag purposeless to the eye,
Witless and teasing, yet
Always beyond my net,
Beyond my fluttering hand that could not fly.
Brave alter-mystery,
Always you found some shadow for your cover.

Or I would watch you trembling on a branch
Open and close with pure control your wings
As if a steady hand
Slowly could wind, unwind
The coil that steeled those frail yet tensile springs,
As if unhurried breathings
Had drifted you aloft out of my reach.

Lost beyond reach—yet still I tried to follow
Down your close paths and into the sun again,
For what except to yield
All pleasures of the field
Into a single, gold and gathered grain?
To force the flash of vision
Under my grasp to fill that pulsing hollow?

And what if I garnered death, the fix of art,
Instead of the moving spark I chose to race?
When winter found my hoard
Pinned to a naked board,
Was it my own long-legged, sidelong grace
I had betrayed, the space
Of instant correspondence in the heart?

2

For there were times, after long hours spent
In meadows smelling hot and dry of noon
Where every grass would stir
Shagged over with blue aster,
I would surprise you, dozing, fumbling drone.
Quickly my sliding prison
Would muffle you in clouds of blinding lint.

And I would pinch my net around that weed
You hung from, until beating up and out
In dense, bewildered strivings
You battered with your wings
And head against the deep net's lightstruck throat,
Or loosening your feet
Crawled up the folded shadows of its side.

Then carrying you as hopefully as an egg
Cradled in cotton, I would pause, advance
On cautious legs until
I found someone to kill
The body I had pinioned in its dance—
Small, ignorant, intense
And homely engine of the whirligig.

Still in odd dreams I ponder, was it strength
Never to bear the final act of prey?
What native cowardice
Clamped me as in a vise
Before the oozing glamor of decay?
Elusive adversary,
I brought no stillness to your labyrinth.

Even the fields that beckoned then seemed wild,
Shimmering with sun-traps and cloud-plays.

I watch as you alight
And the old conquering fright
Fills up my throat. When shall I learn to praise
Tracing you down dark ways
Once more, live butterflies? ablaze, scared child!

                                                    (42–44)

There are forty-seven kinds of birds flashing in and out of Jane Cooper's *The Flashboat*. But I'm not going to write about Cooper's leave-taking herons, or her phoebes insisting "no more elegies!," or her non-strutting rooster refusing to strut through lower-cased Princeton. Today, I'll write about her butterflies.

First, a personal note. Flashback to the 1970s: Jane Cooper, one of my first poetry teachers, was everything I didn't want to be as a poet. She wore wool skirts, sweater sets, and sensible shoes. Her voice was high and fluty. She pronounced the word "sexual" with a liquid x. She didn't smoke. She said "dearie." Her poems had birds in them, and she knew the names of those birds. She told me once that her hope was to someday be considered a "first-rate minor poet."

I was horrified. "I greet you at the beginning of a great career," Emerson wrote to Whitman. How horrible if he had said, "I greet you at the beginning of a minor career." Better to jump, then. Isn't that why Berryman did it? Isn't that why Plath, Sexton, Frank Stanford? Even Lowell, in a way, in his taxi? Even Keats, to come down with that mortal cold, or Rilke, to prick his finger on that rose?

I was convinced, along with my other young genius friends, that if we weren't to be the great poets, we'd rather be dead poets. I think, for so many years after that that it hurts to admit, I actually felt *superior* to Jane. I was still wanting to be the great poet; she was only wanting to be the good one. How wrong I was. I'm glad I lived long enough to understand how wrong.

Re-reading her first book *The Weather of Six Mornings* (1969), I suddenly saw Jane as a young woman, younger than myself when I first knew her, coming into her glory: a marvelous combination of brilliance and bravado, terror and temerity, dressed in sensible shoes.

It's hard enough to write about birds—but butterflies! Sappy Subject Trap Number One for a young woman poet of Jane Cooper's generation, and she certainly knew it. (To know what it was like to be a gifted—ergo, conflicted—young white Southern woman of her time, read her still-important 1974 essay/memoir/

meditation "Nothing Has Been Used in the Manufacture of This Poetry That Could Have Been Used in the Manufacture of Bread.") But Jane will have her butterfly poem (Wordsworth had several!). And like the obedient elusive butterflies that they are, they'll show themselves to us, but they won't stay long. "Monarch and fritillary, swallowtail—": they're the first onstage, and for an instant, they hold their assigned places in a breathless but stately iambic line; they're the center of our attention for three more lines until our speaker races on stage: our little girl poet, chasing beauty.

For three more stanzas, one young girl "of long-legged, sidelong grace" chases butterflies. They disappear into the woods (all the best spiritual journeys start in the first stanza); they coil and uncoil under her gaze like music under a tender microscope (stanza 3), or they disappear into high darkness or wide sunlight, where poetry and philosophy are indivisible (think about stanza 4).

Poets have been chasing beauty for a long time. In "Practicing for Death," Jane Cooper shakes Keats's Grecian urn, and butterflies fly out.

Or I would watch you trembling on a branch. . . .

Jane had been touched, she writes in that essay "Nothing Has Been Used . . . ," by John Crowe Ransom's notion that it is "the specific detail, intimately rendered, that reveals our love for a subject." "Specific" and "intimate" are the key words here. I don't know whether she knew Ransom's words before or after she wrote "Practicing for Death," but no matter. We see and hear it in her, in even her earliest work; it could not have been Ransom who introduced her to the idea, but perhaps he offered her this beautiful and succinct phrasing of what had always been her personal and artistic way of being.

Jane Cooper also had a gorgeous "ear" for poetry. She could hear, and make us hear, what Edith Sitwell called "the texture of words." "Practicing for Death"—if it wasn't so daunting to think of Jane Cooper this way—is a virtuoso performance of playing by that ear and playing by the score. There are the delicious assonances and consonances carrying us along; there are the obvious and not-so-obvious rhymes, half rhymes, internal rhymes and homophones that are part of what keep her lines fluid and surprising, yet feeling inevitable—like the elusive zigzagging of butterflies. She seems to be singing even when she's speaking ("those frail yet tensile springs") and vice-versa ("the deep net's lightstruck throat"). Move over Tennyson, and your innumerable bees; here comes Jane Cooper—listen to all those "air" and "er" sounds droning in summer's late languorous afternoon, insect-whirring heat: "For *there* we*re* times, af*ter* long hours spent / In meadows smelling hot and dry of noon, / *Where* eve*ry* grass would st*ir* / Shagged ov*er* with blue ast*er*, / I would *sur*prise you. . . ."

> And what if I garnered death, the fix of art,
> Instead of the moving spark I chose to race?

I'm old enough now to read Jane Cooper with a new appreciation of her craft, and I'm dutifully embarrassed to see how much I missed noticing when I was younger. But what I've cared about most in her work is not her technical virtuosity; it's her "moving spark."

What makes Jane Cooper an indispensable poet for me is the example of her fine, loyal and "tangled track" in claiming and reclaiming herself as poet, and her openness and generosity in writing about it, in both poetry and prose.

What makes Jane Cooper a necessary poet is that, out of her own conflicts, she managed to create a poetry, a poetics really, of both sacrifice and amplitude. We can build on this, because we have all experienced that conflict within ourselves. She has enlarged what can be written about, spoken about, imagined.

What I love about Jane Cooper's "Practicing for Death" (which is what life is, after all) is the difficult, beautiful question it asks us: How can we, as poets, as people, most adequately, most abundantly, most accurately—without self-congratulation or self-destruction—honor the deepest "correspondences" of our hearts?

We know, by the end of the poem, that Jane managed to nab a few butterflies.

We know, even at the end of her noble life, that Jane was still asking how to turn "pray" into "praise." And "Practicing for Death" is, of course, a prayer.

47

MARIE HOWE

The Story the Surface Cannot Say

IN THE LAST FEW MOMENTS CAME THE OLD GERMAN
CLEANING WOMAN

Our last morning in that long room,
Our little world, I could not cry
But went about the Sunday chores
—Coffee and eggs and newspapers—
As if your plane would never fly,
As if we were stopped there for all time.

Wanting to fix by ritual
The marriage we could never share
I creaked to stove and back again.
Leaves in the stiffening New York sun
Clattered like plates; the sky was bare—
I tripped and let your full cup fall.

Coffee scalded your wrist and that
Was the first natural grief we knew.
Others followed after years:
Dry fodder swallowed, then the tears
When mop in hand the old world through
The door pressed, dutiful, idiot.

(48)

This poem has always stirred me. It's a love poem struck through
with regret—and illuminated by contained rage. Contained in its
rhymed stanzas, as we are constrained in time (the medium of this
poem and the reason for the rage), the utterance quietly presses hard
at its own edges, the surface civil and calm, while a near hysterical
grief is held in and in—until it breaks open like a door.

The rhymes tell the story the surface cannot say. The *room,*
rhymed with *time*—is time, which allows the lovers these last mo-
ments together, and which will separate them for years to come.
That our speaker already knows this (now and then) is what she

suffers. That her *cry*, rhymed with *fly* (which is what her lover is about to do), is unuttered makes it even more loud. And the *chores* linked with *newspapers* intuit what the poem doesn't state— somewhere the world is at war. These times are extreme. The long room is all time. Their domesticity is a temporary make-believe. And the war isn't over: the poet, writing from now looking back to then, is still there. This is the story that still burns in her heart.

In the second stanza, the story within the linked words deepens. What they *share* is *bare*. Naked as lovers, empty as a cupboard, rationed, measured out—fleetingly erotic and gone.

The *ritual* rhymed and ruined with the word *fall* recalls Eve's first separation—why did she drop his full cup? The accident animates what is not allowed to be said: Her rage at him? Her rage at herself? The full cup breaks, although we don't hear that outright—we hear it in our speaker, *creaking* to the stove, in the leaves *stiffening*, and in the *clattered* plates: she is already brittle and old.

But it's the third stanza, perhaps because of the extraordinary containment in the first two, that always makes the hair stand up on my arms. She hurts him ("The coffee scalded your wrist"), wounds him by her stumble (her tripping over the invisible, the unsaid), and the hot coffee falls.

It's then that *knew* is rhymed with *through*. And *tears* with *years*— for they both see and know. As the poet knows—oh, now more than then, which is how the poem turns suddenly fierce, turns against her and time and necessity and the cleaning woman when it rhymes the word *that* with the last word in the poem, *idiot*.

Who is the idiot? The old German cleaning woman surely, dutiful, about to clean up any evidence of their presence together— time itself embodied, knocking at the door. And of course the poet herself, who, speaking with such sudden and uncontained contempt, reveals how deeply the loss has carved a place in her containment. That idiot. The cleaning woman. Herself.

The subliminal poem is what stays with me. The unconscious life of the poem, vivid and newly painful each time I read it. The turn towards self-recrimination—animating, briefly, what might have been, and is not, and never was, and is no more.

LEE UPTON

Jane Cooper
"The Builder of Houses"

Jane Cooper's "The Builder of Houses" is a great and neglected poem—one of the most astute poems about the gendered struggle to be an artist. Repeatedly, I have tried to read the poem's final stanzas as referring to the self-replenishing psyche, the inevitable fading of childhood and the onset of rich maturity. But the poem resists, harboring more rebellious, less comforting sentiments.

First published in *Poetry* in 1958, "The Builder of Houses" was one of Cooper's earliest poems to rely on house imagery. Early and late, houses would come to function in her poetry in radically opposite ways; they are sites of creation, of solitude, the location for an exercise of making—that is, poetry—and, at the same time, they may signify the prospect of devastation.

In "The Builder of Houses," a child erects hideaways that are destroyed, the first time by male cousins, the second by her stepfather who repurposes what she has made into a duck blind for himself. Her next hideaway—a tree house—is discovered by her parents, and the girl is brought down to earth like a "fugitive." Finally, the child creates another small dwelling on an island. Although this shelter goes undiscovered, the poem concludes ambiguously, straddling possibilities.

Does the poem close with a recognition of maturation through love—or with effacement, the probability that conventional love will destroy whatever this "builder of houses" makes in the future? Is the poem about maturity as a process of internalizing earlier structures and destroying our own flimsy self-protective devices? Or is this a poem about exhaustion, in which an incipient artist's new shelter, never quite finished, becomes an imprinted memory of loss and the template for a pattern of unfinished projects?

In the final two stanzas, the poem takes its devastating turn. The girl's hideaway on a "glittering reach" at last goes undiscovered. But it is a "diminished" house, and never completed:

Why was this last, diminished
And never-mentioned mansion
The one she never could finish?
No one—not father nor mother
Nor even the mellowing weather—
Routed her from her chosen foothold and passion;
This time house and view
Were hers, island and vision to wander through.

But less and less she balanced
Her boat on the sunrise water
Or from her window glanced
To where that outline glimmered;
Island and house were inner,
And perhaps existed only for love to scatter
Such long, carefully planned
And sovereign childhood with its unrelenting hand.

(36–37)

Surely we can read the poem's ending as an acknowledgment that imaginative resources must be internalized and childish fortifications destroyed to make way for the complexities of adulthood. As such, adult love must "scatter" the primitive self-protective structures erected in childhood. Yet the poem so carefully mounts its chronicle of threats to creation and self-determination—gendered categories and gendered expectations, appropriations of labor, stifling over-protection—that love in this sequence seems to be yet another antagonist. Cooper's own investment in thinking through the female poet's particular subject position is enclosed within the very grain of the poem. That is, the poem makes turns toward the internalization over time of a diminished sense of the right to claim a voice.

As each house the girl builds will be more precarious, the child must engage in increasing levels of stealth, for she is a maker not only of houses but of secrets and of "her [own] high and forbidden blazing." The poem ends with an image of an "unrelenting hand," circling back to the early image of the girl working with "intent fingers" in the first crucial stirrings of vocation during childhood. As such, while the poem is a record of perils, it is also a chronicle of vocation. After all, the poem's title describes the girl herself; she is "the builder of houses." For the culture in which a woman of Cooper's social class and generation was raised, house-making would have been seen as antithetical to home-making, the latter being an activity that continues to be aligned with gender. As such, the poem is coded with anxiety.

Cooper was candid about her own struggles. In "Nothing Has Been Used in the Manufacture of This Poetry That Could Have Been Used in the Manufacture of Bread" (1974), she conducts a bracing self-audit, chronicling her own struggle to claim the right to be a poet while reconciling her sense of responsibility to others. In the essay, she asks, "Haven't we been most deeply shaped in our very expectations of ourselves, and isn't this what has been most daunting?" (97) She recalls her early failure to finish work; she is not referring to the open networks, the mysterious breathing spaces, the uncapped energy that distinguishes some of her poems published after her first book. Instead, she is referring to her struggle to believe that her own experiences as a woman were material for poetry—and as "The Builder of Houses" dramatizes, she was battling the well-aligned cultural forces that militated against achievement even as early as childhood.

The aesthetic from which "The Builder of Houses" derives depended on refined workmanship: "I wanted everything I wrote to be very fully fleshed out, very finished and exact—I was still working in another tradition."[1] In contrast to this early poem's tightly controlled sound effects, regularity of line lengths, interlocking rhymes, and explanatory material, Cooper will go on in her next collections to develop greater immediacy, a less clotted line, and a deceptively more natural-sounding voice seldom marked with insistent sound echoes. The poems often glide from line grouping to line grouping without necessarily stating or reinforcing an overt connection between images and incidents.

Although situated within her earlier stylistic choices, "The Builder of Houses" suggests a route toward such later poems. As Cooper stated, "I had to get through the perfectionism of those early poems, to learn that no choice is absolute and no structure can save us" (122). Tellingly, the second section of her first book, where the poem appears, is titled "Imaginary Houses"; from the start, she was working out complex conceptual and imagistic structures that rely on the house as a source. Most significantly, "The Builder of Houses" offers up, through its very images, aesthetic strategies that she will move toward: she will go on to construct poems which seem partially dismantled, refusing ultimate closure and suspending logical connections. In a sense, the unfinished final shelter in "The Builder of Houses" is reclaimed for a poetic that discovers in the unfinished a possibility for a renewed conception of what poetry may suggest and enact. Beginning with the later poems of her second book, Cooper's work may no longer be seen as conventionally "finished" in the limited sense—the patina of completion and perfection is now disrupted for a more capacious sense of how conceptual energy may infuse poems. While her houses are rendered in terms of actual physical matter, they are partly, and overtly, immaterial—shot through with dreams and traces of memory. The image of the house—broken into, dismantled, bare, incomplete, suffused with the immaterial—focuses such illuminations.

The development of Cooper's sensibility as it was prefigured by "The Builder of Houses" can be seen progressively in the chronological arrangement of *The Flashboat: Poems Collected and Reclaimed.* The collection reclaims poems that she initially kept out of her earlier books, when she believed such poems were too revealing or too "loosely structured." To reclaim is to judge what had been previously viewed as "unfinished" as newly worthy of attention and preservation. As she writes in the collection's foreword: "If the original self-definitions have been subject to some redefinition, that is part of a lifelong effort to be more honest, to understand a fluid nature in the grip of a difficult century" (19). Her self-characterization as "fluid" is telling even in the context of "The Builder of Houses," for each shelter the girl erects is near water or glazed with water: pond, marsh, icy boards, flooded island. As *The Flashboat* progresses, the poems themselves become more fluid, more ambitiously dreamlike, the syntax more supple, the connections between images and statements less overt.

In 1995, reviewing *Green Notebook, Winter Road* for *Poetry*, Robert B. Shaw noted that "the verbal surface" of Cooper's poems "can seem more provisional than calculatedly final." He goes on to ask, "Why, some might wonder, should we be confronted by something that seems unfinished?" His own judgment is ambiguous: "I can only record the paradox of enjoyment laced with puzzlement and impatience which this book has engendered in me."[2] While his judgment is mixed, his descriptions seem apt for the aesthetic choices that define Cooper's approach. She engages in such effects to duplicate the unfinished and ongoing processes of consciousness, indeed a permeable consciousness that is connected to others and attentive to the residue of violence in history and in personal life.

In some ways, Cooper continually asks how the writer is to live with the anxiety of the half-finished—including cultural conceptions of gender that would make women the incomplete sex, the secondary and less valued sex. One way to explore such questions through poetry would be to reimagine what it is to be unfinished, to reject the seemingly fully enclosed, to reclaim what had been appropriated or wrecked, to respect what is "ruined." As she continued to develop as a poet, she would loosen her earlier constraints, revealing the scaffolding of conceptions, dissolving her structures by creating greater flexibility in her syntactical choices, allowing not only the tangible but the intangible to leave traces on her poems.

Asked to identity her themes, Cooper includes "A sense that our experience includes our dreams as much as our daylight lives."[3] As such, it is useful when reading a poet so influenced by and enamored of dreams to turn to Gaston Bachelard, who wrote compellingly of both dreams and houses and whose work was often circulated among writers of Cooper's generation. Bachelard speculates:

> Maybe it is a good thing for us to keep a few dreams of a house that we shall live in later, always later, so much later, in fact, that we shall not have time to achieve it. For a house that was final, one that stood in symmetrical relation to the house we were born in, would lead to thoughts—serious, sad thoughts—and not to dreams. It is better to live in a state of impermanence than in one of finality.[4]

I bring Bachelard to bear on this discussion because Cooper's poems that return to house imagery in her later career increasingly present the house as a charged space characterized by "unfinished objects on clean shelves," as in "All These Dreams" (145). The "unfinished" becomes both a vital attribute of houses and a way to view poems as dynamic structures that disclose new meanings and dislodge outworn conceptions.

Cooper explicitly draws from house imagery that collides with dream imagery in "Ordinary Detail." The poem begins, "I'm trying to write a poem that will alert me to my real life" and continues with a sequence of common images: breakfast dishes, yogurt, napkins, a friend reading a letter. The poem then opens to "the unseen":

> Last night the girl dreamed of a triple-locked door
> at the head of a short flight of steps. Why couldn't she get in?

How to take possession of that room? Will it be hers to keep?

Remembering, she loses track of her sentence, frowns suddenly,
   smiles,
excusing herself to the others. A friend's brother died of AIDS.
Sensuality is not the secret; it's more like redemption, or
   violence. . . .
The girl is walking furiously, under a mild, polluted sky.

                                                                    (174)

Here, as in "The Builder of Houses," we have a young girl who
questions if she can enter and possess a place of her own. The con-
cluding stanza, however, turns toward physical threat. As a life-long
sufferer from a form of immune deficiency that was not acquired,
Cooper's sympathy and identification with those suffering from
AIDS marks the poem. Here, the house—repeated with such con-
sistency in her work—is allied with the body as a primary defining
structure, as we are "housed" bodily. Given the vulnerability of
houses as she presents them, we may register an echo of Cooper's
heightened sense of the physical body's fragility. As she writes in
"The Past":

And how do I connect in my own body—that is, through touch—
the War of 1812 with the smart rocket nosing its way via CNN
down a Baghdad street? How much can two arms hold? How soon
will my body, which already spans a couple of centuries, become
almost transparent and begin to shiver apart?

                                                                    (202)

To be a house builder is to design and construct—to declare one's
ability to respond to containing structures, whether house or poem
or body—and to acknowledge that we may control less than we
may have first supposed. While Adrienne Rich's influential poem
"Diving into the Wreck" narrates a descent into the ruins of ideol-
ogy, in Cooper's poetry, the wreck isn't to be descended into; the
wreck surrounds us; the wreck, precarious and vulnerable, is already
with us.

In an interview, Cooper described her desire to make poems capa-
ble of gathering the accumulated insight of each period of her life:
"I just think that if you can write so that every stage of your life

makes its own contribution, has its own wisdom—that's wonderful, it's a wonderful gift."[5]

To read her poetry at this point in the twenty-first century may mean to recognize her poems as predictive in ways that go beyond even her own initial projections, for the house, as a place of privacy harboring the artist's growth, appears more elusive than ever. Privacy, after all, is a declining resource, as the technological means to monitor private spaces accelerates. Like the girl in "The Builder of Houses," our hideaways are always in danger of being found out.

Cooper's poetry continues to resonate with and to disclose questions that defy accepted answers. How to inhabit a life, how to make a place to be inhabited, how to secure the conditions for understanding our lives, what to make of the unfinished: these are the issues that animate Cooper as early as "The Builder of Houses." They are not issues we are likely to finish with ourselves.

Notes

1. Cooper, "An Interview with Jane Cooper." With Eric Gudas. *The Iowa Review* 25, no. 1 (1995): 105.

2. Robert B. Shaw. Review of *For That Day Only*, by Grace Shulman and *Green Notebook, Winter Road*, by Jane Cooper. *Poetry* (May 1995): 107.

3. Cooper, "Interview with Jane Cooper," *The Iowa Review*, 98.

4. Gaston Bachelard. *The Poetics of Space.* Trans. Maria Jolas. (Boston: Beacon Press, 1994): 61.

5. Cooper, "Interview with Jane Cooper," *The Iowa Review*, 110.

ERIC GUDAS

Jane Cooper's "Reclaimed" Poems

In July of 1994, I interviewed Jane Cooper about her first full-length book in decades, *Green Notebook, Winter Road,* whose publication was to coincide with her seventieth birthday in October of that year. With her characteristic meticulousness, Cooper insisted on selecting, editing, and ordering my questions before I arrived at her apartment on the Upper West Side. In fact, Cooper herself wrote the following question, which wasn't on my short-list at all: "On the question of scope, you're a writer who, despite a lifelong, passionate commitment to poetry, has published only about a hundred poems in four books. Could you comment on that?"[1] Proud as she clearly felt of the *Green Notebook* poems, Cooper's answer to her own question shows she was worrying over the shape and size of her oeuvre as a whole:

> Lately, I've been going through old boxes of poems and poem-drafts . . . [and] I was startled to find that there are probably a couple of hundred more poems that have never been published. A lot of them shouldn't have been published—those decisions were perfectly sound. But some are quite decent, and I don't know what to do about them. It's very odd to consider publishing a *Collected Poems* that would include old poems that have never been seen before! You want to be concerned with what will happen next, not with what you did in some kind of silence twenty or thirty years ago. Still, even I believe that I've made something a bit larger than can be found on the library shelf.[2]

Over the years, I've kicked myself for not asking more follow-up questions to a statement that now seems like a bombshell to me. It's not every day a major American poet reveals she has only published one-third of the poems she has written. Since many of my favorites among her older poems appeared in the "Reclaimed Poems: 1954–1969" section of *Scaffolding: New and Selected Poems* (1984), I don't know why I didn't jump at the chance to hear about more unpub-

57

lished poems. There's also an ambivalence in Cooper's tone that I wish I'd probed. On the one hand, she half-chastises herself for her preoccupation with manuscripts from previous decades. On the other hand, she intimates that those very manuscripts might bolster her reputation (a word that she herself uses nowhere in the interview) in an almost physical way by increasing the space her work would take "on the library shelf."

Over the next few years, Cooper overcame this ambivalence enough to assemble *The Flashboat: Poems Collected and Reclaimed* (2000). She made the process of sifting through her manuscripts a prominent part of the book itself by adding "reclaimed" to the subtitle and including about twenty of the unpublished poems she'd alluded to in our interview by "insert[ing] them in the rough chronology of the published work" (19), thereby changing the very shape of her books as they'd originally appeared. In *Scaffolding*, on the other hand, she had annexed the "reclaimed" poems within the separate section I just mentioned. Between the two collections, Cooper published almost twenty-five "reclaimed" poems—that is, about one-eighth of the unpublished poems she referred to in our interview. Cooper's initial definition of "reclaimed" poems in *The Flashboat*'s foreword—"poems that could have been part of earlier books but were left out"—is so neutral it begs to be read metaphorically, especially "left out" (19). The "reclaimed" poems, especially those from the 1950s and '60s, put back in some of what seems "left out" of Cooper's published work: namely, a more direct and assertive "I"; a stronger emphasis on relations between actual people, and not simply one person and a mentally apostrophized or wholly imagined other; a wider range of emotions, including aggression and sexual passion; a looser, less perfectionistic feel in the verse itself; and the vivid sense of a speaking voice.

In fact, many of the "reclaimed" poems from the 1950s and '60s outshine their published counterparts in *The Weather of Six Mornings* so brightly, it's hard not to wonder if they would have won her more readers if she'd published them when she first wrote them. In *The Flashboat,* Cooper admits that "when such poems were omitted [from earlier books], it was because they seemed too personal, at other times because they were rather loosely written" (19). Rather than analyze such open-ended terms as "personal" and "loose" in the abstract, I'd like to ground this statement in one of my favorite poems of Cooper's, "All the Leaves Were Green," written sometime in the early to mid-1960s and "reclaimed" for *The Flashboat*:

Darling, I had my hand on your khaki
knee, the air was shining, the murmur
of small summer grass and insects came in
through the car window. You were saying,
no, singing that theme from Bach, "hung up"
on its repetitions, smiling, unfaltering.
Then was it me beside you in the dark wet
Virginia night when, a curve missed, the wall
smashed into your windshield? O was it me
you saved with a last wrench of will, your hand
white and square on the wheel, my childish
mouth open and screaming?

(56)

From "Darling" to "screaming," this two-lines-short-of-a-sonnet
hurtles forward headlong from quiet but passionate affection to
violent death, heedless of many of the rules Cooper observes in
other poems of the period. Or perhaps it would be more accurate
to say that the poem—through its setting in a car—superimposes
the moments of love and death atop each other, so they take place
almost simultaneously. Just as the poem's speaker seems to implicate
herself in a crash for which she wasn't actually present, so the po-
em's heavy use of enjambment and precipitous syntax—the first
sentence is a run-on and, in contrast to most poems of Cooper's
from this era, there is nary a semi-colon in sight—speeds the poem
inexorably along towards the curve and the speaker's violent cry. Yet
the poem's first half, although it participates in this formal reckless-
ness, evokes a quietly sensuous moment almost out of time. The
poem's title, as well as the evocations of "air," "grass," and "insects,"
set the poem in spring or summer, those seasons associated with
youth and renewal. Almost all of the action described is in some
way cyclical—certainly the natural details, but also the "repetitions"
of the Bach piece that preoccupy the beloved.

What about the poem would have seemed "too personal" to
Cooper? She composed it at, or not long after, a time when "chil-
dren, landscapes, [and] old men" predominated in her poems; and
whereas she treats these subjects—all of them presumably safe—as
archetypes, the subject of "All the Leaves Were Green" seems like an
actual person, evoked through his "khaki[s]," his beloved Bach, and
especially through quoted half-colloquial syntax—that memorable
"'hung up'" (56). (I'm reminded of the luminous and almost wholly
unexplained concrete details used as a method of characterization

by modernist fiction writers like Katherine Mansfield, to whom Cooper pays homage in another poem.) And of course he is a lover, and if Cooper wrote many love poems, she published very few, and those she did—"Pencil Sketch of Self & Other," for instance, whose speaker remembers how she and a lover "almost ruined each other"—evoke failed or thwarted love affairs (139). Nothing about "All the Leaves Were Green," however, suggests failure: only the "curve missed" comes between the lovers, and even that the speaker tries to redeem by imagining herself beside her lover when he dies. That last detail, "my childish / mouth open and screaming," seems personal because it evokes such violent feeling. But isn't there also a hint of sexual abandon in the self-description? It's almost as if because the speaker can't, or won't, portray lovemaking in the first six lines, that erotic power returns nonetheless in the second section. This slippage between sexual passion and violent death in the poem's two sections may have made this a dangerously personal poem for its writer to publish.

Cooper embedded bits of "All the Leaves Were Green" within her sequence "The Weather of Six Mornings," which, despite keen, sympathetic readings by other poets, has always left me rather cold. Unlike the former poem, it's very controlled, a meditation on speechlessness. The beloved addressed so passionately elsewhere seems a faraway, archetypal figure in the published poem: "Hearing of your death / by a distant roadside // I wanted to erect some marker" (60). Contrast that "distant roadside" with the almost morbidly sensuous and certainly more specific "dark wet / Virginia night" (56). Only a few lines of "Weather of Six Mornings" approach the lushness of its unpublished double, as when its speaker refers to a distant future time when "I can speak of your living, // the lightning-flash of meeting, / the green leaves waving at our windows" (61). Compared with the heedlessness of "All the Leaves Were Green," however, these lines seem positively anemic. The latter poem's phrase, "the air was shining," for instance, goes beyond the literal as "green leaves [were] waving," in the published poem, does not. Yet reading the two poems alongside each other, as *The Flashboat* compels us to, adds depth and poignancy to "The Weather of Six Mornings," whose speaker laments the difficulty of speech and writing: "I try to speak / of what is so hard for me" and "Words knock at my breast, / heave and struggle to get out" (58, 59). After reading "All the Leaves Were Green," it's easy to see (or at least to speculate) that intense—and intensely mingled—grief and eroticism were among the subjects trapped inside the speaker of "The Weather of Six Mornings."

"Blind Girl," which Cooper wrote in 1954, but first published three decades later in *Scaffolding*, also deals with a speaker who is in some way blocked—in this case, literally blocked off from the world (as she says) "called outside" (29).[3] A dramatic monologue addressed to the speaker's beloved or close friend, the poem articulates frankly tender and destructive impulses absent from many other Cooper poems of this era; in fact, the intertwining of tenderness and aggression lends the poem its transgressive *frisson*. Written in loose blank verse, "Blind Girl" recalls what critic Robert Burns calls "the deliberate roughenings of the iambic pentameter line . . . in Frost, Yeats, Thomas, and Graves," whose "common aim was to move away from the elaborately musical effects of [Victorian poets] to something convincingly like speech."[4] In contrast with Cooper's published poems of this era with their elaborate syntax, "Blind Girl" uses short, pointed sentences, as in the opening: "I take your hand. I want to touch your eyes. / They are water-soft. I know. I could push them in." These five brief, urgent sentences are driven by the first person as few other poems in Cooper's work at the time are. Whereas "The Weather of Six Mornings," written a few years later, uses "I" five times in sixty lines, "Blind Girl" uses it nine times in its twenty-one lines—and four times in the first two lines alone. It's not merely the prevalence of "I" in "Blind Girl" that distinguishes it from Cooper's other poems, but the sense of a desperate, urgent speaking voice and of a self longing to assert itself. Almost all of the five verbs in the poem's opening lines are grammatically linked to the speaking "I." Of course the most unsettling verb is "push," as in "push them in," which articulates an impulse so violent it verges on the murderous.

At the same time, Cooper the poet shows a willingness—not exactly to murder the blank verse norm that her first line, with its five iambs, introduces, but certainly to vary the pattern quite aggressively with the addition of extra syllables in the second line. The result is a disorienting mixture of anapests and iambs out of which the accented syllables—including "push" and "in"—surge. Perhaps "Blind Girl" possesses such aural power because Cooper wishes to de-emphasize the visual throughout and to emphasize senses like touch and hearing on which her blind speaker relies—even if those senses do not console her for her missing sight. Here, the speaker implicitly compares herself to two empty objects:

Once a doll's eyes fell in before my fingers—
Instead of dropping tick-tock open and shut
They were cold holes like a poor frozen faucet.
Where does the water come from? I hear breathing.
Listen at the tap—you hear a kind of sobbing.

The blank verse once again—although not as dramatically as in line two—exemplifies what Cooper called the "loosely written" quality that may have caused her to embargo the poem, but which I see as daring experimentation within an established verse form. Note the run of lines that begin with trochees, the anapests, and the accented syllables jammed up against each other—most dramatically "cold holes." Speaking of the "holes"—earlier I said that two objects in these lines (the doll's eye sockets and the faucet) were empty but not quite. Each contains the possibility of fullness just out of reach; or, rather, what is absent from each object—eyes, running water—constitutes a maddening semi-presence for the speaker. Her sightlessness chills like ice, but the eyes of her sighted companion she longs to touch have "light"—and therefore warmth—"in them, asking to get let out."

Jean Valentine once evoked Melville in writing about Cooper, whose "truest subject," she claimed, "is not intellectual liberation only, but liberation as passionate as Ahab's."[5] I begin to see a bit of Ahab's ferocious, hate-filled egotism in "Blind Girl," whose ending echoes the Captain's always-resonant question, which Valentine quotes, "How can the prisoner reach outside except by thrusting through the wall?"[6] The blind girl, too, is a prisoner for whom the entire world—even her human companion—is a wall that traps her and separates her from what she lacks—which, of course, includes sight (or "seeing," in the poem's more active parlance) but is not limited to the sensory or even the tangible. In the poem's conclusion, she articulates an almost Ahab-like desire to get at, or even beyond, "seeing":

I take your hand. There. Please let me hold you.
If I hold tight enough to your live fingers
It *must* work free. Oh, I could kill your eyes
Only to know a little more what love is.

Eschewing the elaborate diction and syntax of her published poems—and indeed, for increased drama, of other sections in this poem—Cooper relies here almost solely on monosyllabic words and short sentences to create a sense of mingled tenderness, desperation, and destructiveness. "There" and "Oh" add to the poem's spoken quality, although whether the speaker truly addresses her companion or whether she remains trapped in self-address is hard to decide. What she speaks *about* is hard to apprehend, too, in part because of that maddeningly vague "it," which might refer to "seeing"; but "live fingers" (could the blind girl be a zombie?) implies that the speaker is after something even more basic than her missing sense. Whatever "it" embodies, the speaker's willingness to "kill" for it makes her a threatening figure, even if the threat seems poised to redound on her. It's not so much the promised violence itself that makes the blind girl so aggressive as her willingness to express it. She does not live in a world where "the self is . . . no more important than anybody else" (as Cooper characterized the world of *The Weather of Six Mornings*, 98). Instead, she embodies a sense of self-importance so potent—if also poignant, stemming, as it seems to, from a deep sense of injury and lack—that it threatens to devour the speaker, her interlocutor, or both, in the rush toward "love."

I'm sorry Sylvia Plath didn't get to read "Blind Girl," which anticipates the more flamboyantly aggressive and self-destructive female speakers of *Ariel*, almost a decade before those poems were written. But Cooper let the poem languish "in some kind of silence" for thirty years before bringing it out it in *Scaffolding* and, later, in *The Flashboat*. In the end, Cooper's inclusion of the "reclaimed" poems didn't make *The Flashboat* into a much bigger book than it would have been without them (especially since she omitted some published poems), belying her self-revelatory claim I quoted earlier: "even I believe that I've made something a bit larger than can be found on the library shelf." And yet, as Cooper well knew, "larger" has many denotations, not all of which have to do with physical size. *The Flashboat* contains multitudes. Poems like "All the Leaves Were Green" and "Blind Girl" impart a greater sense of Cooper's range, both technical and emotional, than do many of the poems she chose to publish at the time. They anticipate the more expansive poet she became in her fifties and sixties. They rank among the best poems she wrote at any point in her career, which means they belong among the best lyric poems by any American poet in the second half of the twentieth century. Although she wrote them before the women's movement of the late 1960s and early '70s "enabled [her] to speak of what once seemed incommunicable," they show she was plumbing the depths of the barely articulable as early as the 1950s (and, as the "Mercator's World" poems show, even earlier) along with many of her female peers, albeit in isolation (20). And now—since she published no more books after *The Flashboat*—their appearance, belated but no less vital, so many years after she wrote and then consigned them to boxes, has become a gesture of farewell.

Notes

1. Eric Gudas and Jane Cooper. "An Interview with Jane Cooper." *The Iowa Review* 25, no. 1 (Winter 1995): 106.

2. Ibid., 91, 107.

3. All subsequent references to "Blind Girl" also come from page 29 and will not be cited in text.

4. Robert Burns Shaw, *Blank Verse: A Guide to Its History and Use* (Athens: Ohio University Press, 2007), 113.

5. Jean Valentine, dust jacket comment (a.k.a. blurb) on Cooper's *Green Notebook, Winter Road* (Gardiner, Maine: Tilbury House, 1994).

6. Herman Melville, *Moby-Dick, or, The Whale* 150th anniversary ed. (New York: Penguin, 2001), 178.

CLARE ROSSINI

"In the Grip of a Difficult Century"
Personal and Cultural History in Cooper's Maps & Windows

In the spring of 1980, Jane Cooper was in residence at the University of Iowa, and I was lucky enough to be assigned to her workshop. Our class met in Cooper's apartment, where tall windows brought in extravagant amounts of light. As my classmates and I trundled in for our first meeting, we found a table set with cookies, fruit, cheese, and a big pot of espresso coffee; a teapot was singing on the stove. That semester, my fellow students and I quickly learned that Cooper nurtured her students, body and soul. Pedagogically, she was a minimalist, giving us plenty of room to argue about the merits of worksheet poems before she'd come in with a question or insight that would suddenly clarify the issue at hand or nudge the conversation in another, more productive direction. Not one for professorial pronouncements, Cooper taught us to articulate each poem's implicit formal and thematic ambitions and to go from there. Her quiet, open-ended approach shaped that workshop like none other I've been in. Students who'd rarely spoken in other classes piped up; the cloud of embattled egotism—which so often eclipses learning in a workshop situation—lifted, then vanished altogether. Years later, in the *sturm und drang* of my own workshops, I still find myself attempting to emulate Cooper, to teach with that light, firm touch.

That same semester, I set about reading Cooper's two books: *The Weather of Six Mornings,* published in 1969 and winner of the Lamont Prize, and *Maps & Windows*, a collection of new and selected poems published in 1974. I remember the experience of reading these books vividly—remember, too, the sense of surprise and dislocation that came as I moved from the first to the second. I'd like to retrace that readerly experience here because, having just re-read Cooper's five full-length books and having the luxury of seeing the work as a whole, I feel keenly that her aptly titled second book is key to understanding her evolving sense of the poetic enterprise. *Maps & Windows* is a book of big gestures. It draws on a complex mix of personal and cultural history to show a poet who has adopted "a lifelong effort to be more honest, to understand a fluid nature in the grip of a difficult century" (19).

When I opened Cooper's first book in February 1980, I found a poet whose early work, like that of many in her generation, was written in traditional forms. The poems were lushly sensual, capable of rendering intimate moments with a subtle erotic throb:

> And take that moment when your flame-blue eyes
> Blazed on me till true sunlight seemed to fail
> And all our landscape fell away like lies:
> The burr of bees, grass, flowers, the slow sundial.

> (45)

To wield the line with such authority, to conjure a moment with language both precise and allusive: as a new poet looking to refine her craft, I remember being dazzled by poems like these.

A handful of poems in *Weather* attend to the poet's intimacies with a male lover. But many more are elegiac, exploring the poet's grief when the beloved is killed. In "March," for example, the poet returns "little by little / to the rooms where we slept, the closet / where you hung your worn raincoat" (67). In "The Faithful," the poet wakens to see a ghost of the beloved, "A shape dissolving and flittering / Unsteady as a flame in a draft house" (28). *The Weather of Six Mornings* widens beyond the lover's death to explore other species of loss and negation. A poem about childhood, for example, is titled "Practicing for Death." References to dreams and ghosts are scattered throughout, for "death is my old friend who waits on the stairs" (52). Even a moment of transcendence is figured in language that leans toward dissolution: in "Rock Climbing," the poet arrives "At the lost line where wind is turned to water / And all is turned to light, dissolved or rinsed / To silver . . ." (33).

Elegiac poetry often aspires to a sense of timelessness. In Cooper's first collection, this effect is created in part by repeated references to the ongoing cycles of weather and the seasons. In "March," for example, all but one of the eight sections are clearly set in very early spring, whose winds and precipitation color the poem's atmosphere. Section four of the title poem connects the possibility of speech itself to the end of a rainy stretch: "If the weather breaks / I can speak of your dying, / if the weather breaks, / if the crows stop calling / and flying low" (61). The fact of human mortality set against the cyclical patterns of the natural world creates the fruitful tension at the heart of *The Weather of Six Mornings*. Yet the book ends on a skeptical note, as if questioning the poet's enterprise: "To the sea of received silence // why should I sign / my name?" (63). Re-reading Cooper's first book, I felt that question reverberate back through the collection, interrogating it, as if the poet intuited the revisionary spirit of her next work.

When I read *Maps & Windows: Selected Poems* later that semester, I was surprised and at first taken aback by what lay between the covers of this slim paperback. I thought I *knew* this poet, had grasped her project. But Cooper's second book parted company from her first with such insistence that I felt I was meeting the poet for the first time. *Maps & Windows* may be the most complex of Cooper's books, in part because it contains so many different types of work: poems from her first collection; new work; a long, rich, historically and personally revelatory essay; and a final section of poems from a manuscript Cooper had written in her twenties, nearly a quarter-century before. Then and now, a reader must sort out the relationships among these versions of the poet, this range of form and subject and voice. If the book seems something of a patchwork, it's a potent one. In time, I came to appreciate the gutsiness of *Maps & Windows*, the way it reveals a poet in a moment of bold redefinition. But first, I had to get to know *this* Jane Cooper.

Maps & Windows opens with a section titled "Calling Me from Sleep: New and Selected Poems 1961–1973." A handful of poems in the section are reprinted from Cooper's first book, but with subtle changes. "March," for example, is represented by only five of its original eight sections, each printed separately, with its own title; the sequence itself is dissolved. A previously unpublished poem, "Letters," is slipped in, a poem that frankly acknowledges the poet's physical intimacy with an unnamed lover: "Darling, my white body / still bears your imprint" (57). Small changes, yes, but I already had an impression of Cooper as a meticulous poet for whom every compositional choice would be carefully weighed. Had she found the excised sections of "March" less true to the emotional realities behind the poem? Was "Letters" meant to reveal a more passionate and willful self? In the context of the rest of the book, such assertions seem valid. It is interesting to note that the *Weather* selection in *Maps & Windows* opens not with an elegiac poem, as does the original collection, but with "My Young Mother," which ends with the poet hearing her mother "calling me from sleep after decades" (53). The line seems thematically urgent: some long-absent female energy is calling the poet to wakening and renewal.

Following the *Weather* section, *Maps & Windows* moves to new work written in the late sixties and early seventies. Many of these poems represent a clear break, formally speaking, from those in Cooper's first book. Stanzas are often irregular in length, and lines in some of the poems are long enough to read like musical prose. The language is frequently colloquial, as in "Suicide Note," where the speaker begins almost petulantly—"It's not that I'm out of touch— / a child stranded on a shoal"— and moves toward an exasperated "It's just that everyone else's / needs seem so urgent!" *The Weather of Six Mornings* contained almost no dialogue. In contrast, the new poems of *Maps & Windows* include the voices of Rilke's Malte Laurids Brigges; of a suburbanite, talking to herself; and of a pair of lovers wakened by an earthquake. "*You pushed me out of bed!*" one accuses the other before they "start to laugh": lines that bring Cooper's wry sense of humor into her work for the first time ("The Earthquake," 138). This and other new poems seem to spring from particular moments: "When you kissed me it was as if / someone had just stepped lightly out the room" ("Pencil Sketch of Self & Other," 139).

Given the immediacy of the new work in *Maps & Windows*, it's not surprising to find that these poems' subjects are often grounded in the social and cultural realities of their time. Yet reading *The Weather of Six Mornings* and *Maps & Windows* in sequence, I felt again the surprise of history's sudden emergence in the work. History—and politics, too. In "A Nightmare of the Suburbs," Cooper depicts the racist paranoia which underlay "white flight" out of America's core cities in the 1960s and early 1970s (137). In "Waiting," the poet speaks lovingly to her "old body, old friend" about the fact it will not bear children (140). The women's movement of the sixties and seventies, with its emphasis on broadening choices and roles for women, clearly is in the air of this poem.

The shift in Cooper's work from the quiet formalism of the *Weather* poems to the porous, open-ended, time-conscious new poems: this was the first surprise of *Maps & Windows*. The second was the book's middle section, titled "Nothing Has Been Used in the

Manufacture of This Poetry That Could Have Been Used in the Manufacture of Bread" and consisting of a twenty-nine-page essay.

"Nothing Has Been Used . . ." is a personally revelatory work in which Cooper looks back to her life as a young woman poet in Princeton, New Jersey, in the years during and after World War II. A work with historical as well as literary importance, "Nothing Has Been Used" is crucial in understanding Cooper's life and ambitions. The central revelation of "Nothing Has Been Used" is that *The Weather of Six Mornings* is Cooper's *second* full-length work; her first, written during and just after the war years, was the manuscript of "'a book of war poems from a woman's point of view'" (102–3). Cooper speaks of this period as a time in which she deeply felt both the tragic nature of the war and the exuberance of a young artist making her first work: "I was . . . learning to know myself and others, learning my craft of poetry, all my senses were opening" (106). When the war ends, Cooper studies at Oxford, where she learns that poetry was read in the London bomb shelters, a fact that affirms both the subjects she writes about and the power of art itself: "For the first time poetry presented itself to me as a means of survival" (100).

Meanwhile, Princeton was filled with veterans back from the war who were working on their college degrees, and when Cooper returns home, she falls in love more than once, an experience both exhilarating and difficult. The young poet struggles to reconcile her creative ambitions with the expectations of a long-term relationship, especially in a time in which marriage seemed to have but one clear end: "most of my friends wanted three or four babies as soon as they could afford them" (106).

Looking back in the fifties and sixties, Cooper remembers her first manuscript as focusing on her personal experience of the war. But, as she writes in "Nothing Has Been Used," she is surprised to discover years later that over half the poems in the manuscript explore the increasingly fraught connection between the poet-self and the potential wife and mother, a struggle Cooper describes as "the doubleness of my urge to become" (108). The pain of this "doubleness," she says, is exacerbated by a culture in which to be a woman poet—as a fellow male poet tells her—was "a contradiction in terms"; women were barely represented in journals and anthologies, and role models were equally scarce (108). In the early fifties, Cooper begins her teaching career at Sarah Lawrence. She takes two years off to attend the Iowa Writers Workshop, where, the only woman in a class of twelve, she studies with Lowell and Berryman. As Cooper's professional life comes together, she begins writing and publishing the poems that would form the core of *The Weather of Six Mornings*. Meanwhile, the manuscript of her early twenties, its poems written out of an internal and seemingly intractable conflict, is abandoned.

In the early 1970s, Cooper finds herself writing poems that seem to be "getting back to something closer to the mood of my earliest work." She begins to pore over the unpublished manuscript, selecting fifteen poems to appear in "Mercator's World," the fourth section of *Maps & Windows*.

Reading these feisty, restless, proto-feminist poems again, I remember the surprise of encountering them, and then of realizing that *The Weather of Six Mornings* was written in their shadow. In the first poem, "Eve," the protagonist, knows she must marry; otherwise, the snake will have her whole, including that most private part, her imagination, "her sky / No one else shares" (78). That's some gutsy revision of the Judeo-Christian creation myth, one clearly at odds with the prevailing values of the late 1940s. Other poems reverberate with anger. In "Long View from the Suburbs," Cooper describes a male poet who sets up a date but doesn't show up, revealing later that he spent the time working on a new poem. "Long View" ends with a striking image of the poet's frustration and despair:

> . . . Do you know, young man,
> Do they teach you in biographies
> How it feels to open like a city
> At the caress of darkness, then sickening
> To walk about alone
> Until a streetlamp yawns in reckoning?
>
> (87)

Many of the "Mercator's World" poems show the young poet's anguish as she tries to sustain her creative life in a period during which women's roles in American society were becoming increasingly codified and limited. One wonders, as Cooper does in "Nothing Has Been Used," how this first manuscript would have been received had she published it closer to the time she wrote the poems, a decade before the first stirrings of the women's movement.

Cooper's historical consciousness permeates every section of *Maps & Windows*. It is implicit in the revisions and re-orderings of the *Weather* poems and explicit in the form and often the subjects of the new work. As I hope the discussion above makes clear, the complex relationship of personal and cultural history is the deep subject of "Nothing Has Been Used." But Cooper's recognition of history as a self-defining force is perhaps most dramatically revealed in her inclusion here of the "Mercator's World" section, which ends *Maps & Windows*. By choosing to publish poems from this first, abandoned manuscript, Cooper makes clear that thinking historically means publically declaring not only what one *is,* but what one has been. Cooper will come to call this gesture "reclamation," a notion she refers to in her fourth book, *Scaffolding: New and Selected Poems,* where a section of previously unpublished work is called "Reclaimed Poems," and in the title of her final publication: *The Flashboat: Poems Collected and Reclaimed.*

Cooper's sense of history continued to invigorate her poetic practice. I'll point toward just two broadly illustrative examples. *Green Notebook, Winter Road,* Cooper's fourth collection, contains prose and poems that draw on her Florida childhood, including portraits and stories of ancestors, relatives, and family lore, all of which offer ways to "relish yet redress / my sensuous, precious, upper-class / unjust white child's past" (190). The phrase "relish yet redress" makes clear that the poet comes at her memories with an understanding of how an individual life can reflect and project larger cultural realities such as racism and classism. That historical consciousness comes to its fullest rendering in work Cooper publishes in *Scaffolding* and *Green Notebook,* in sequences based on the lives and work of Rosa Luxemburg, Georgia O'Keefe, and Willa Cather. These long, lush, exploratory poems, with their broken sentences and patches of prose, open Cooper's work beyond the lyrical "I" into communal history. Tethered to time, the poet may nonetheless use her art to reach through history, connecting to the spirit of other women, other creators.

"Always I have been more interested in the role of time in a writer's work than in any given theme," Cooper says in her foreword to *The Flashboat* (20). Perhaps no aspect of *Maps & Windows* more vividly asserts that focus than Cooper's inclusion of a date at the end of each poem, whether the poem is new, reprinted, or reclaimed. Cooper never uses this device again in her books; it is particular to *Maps & Windows.* The dating seems a pointed gesture, making clear the poems are meant to be read as time-bound documents which allow us to enter "a dialogue with history and otherness" (21). From this point forward, Cooper sees her work as inextricably linked to her life and historical moment. Her task is to explore that link, or—to quote again Cooper's lyrical description of her poetic vocation—"to understand a fluid nature in the grip of a difficult century" (19).

LEE BRICCETTI

Maps & Windows

Like any high-stakes detective story, there is a body. The circumstances of its disposal and discovery are voiced in poem after poem of Jane Cooper's second book, *Maps & Windows*.

A long essay at the center of the book creates an expository bridge from the poetic "present" circa 1974, when *Maps & Windows* was published, through a personal narrative that leads to the revelation of the body. The body is a body of work, a book Cooper had written and suppressed more than twenty years earlier. That book is recovered in the last section of *Maps & Windows* as "Mercator's World: Poems 1947–1951"—and the whole troubling, beautiful project speaks unsparingly about the unstable territory of the poet's development, which is to say her struggle, a woman's struggle, to *be* the poet.

Maps & Windows was assembled during the women's movement and recovers the poet's unpublished, book-length manuscript that had been abandoned in an old Christmas card box. If we believe what we read in the essay—and we do—the manuscript was literally forgotten. What is the agency of forgetting a body of work? What is the historical and psychological crisis that might allow for this? And finally, why should we read it now?

Cooper's first published volume, *The Weather of Six Mornings,* had won the Lamont Poetry prize in 1968, judged by Hayden Carruth, Donald Hall, Donald Justice, William Stafford, and James Wright. *Maps & Windows* came six years later in 1974, establishing Cooper's career-long practice of reshaping and remastering the sequencing of her poems as an act of recovery. Poems from *The Weather of Six Mornings* reappear and are regrouped in *Maps & Windows,* then re-shuffled later in *The Flashboat: Poems Collected and Reclaimed.* Poems salvaged from this first appearance of "Mercator's World" re-emerge later in her publishing history.

Maps & Windows remains the foundational text in Cooper's oeuvre and a map to the rest of her work. It charts a course to self-possession with genre-bending frankness, speaking as poetry collection, prose memoir, and survival manual. It is a highly metonymic work of art, self-aware, both a recovered text and a stand-in for other buried books—and for the books *unwritten* by other women.

Maps & Windows also performs the body in time, creating a dramatic frame for the poet to look at herself and the reader from the vantage point of her past. Given Cooper's careful, encrypted lyric lines, one might not think of Walt Whitman. But since this creation requires the reader to understand the self-conscious agency that put it together over elapsed-time and since it posits self-making as subject, I feel compelled to make a connection to *Song of Myself*. Do I over-reach? Very well. Though she never hoists herself into position as "representative woman" the way Whitman made himself every man, the central essay with the vertiginously long title is confidently aware that it will be read as a witness to a specific time and place—and it takes pains to record the weight and temperament of the post-World War II nation for women writers. Teaching is consciously part of the book's assumptive work, and it understands itself as an oracular document that reaches toward future audiences.

In a profoundly self-regulated opening, *Maps & Windows* begins with the poem "My Young Mother" (which also appeared in *The Weather of Six Mornings*): "My young mother, her face narrow / and dark with unresolved wishes. . . ."[1] The last line of the poem becomes a *cri de coeur* of the entire project and the awakening book: *calling me from sleep after decades.* Cooper's overt augury and *call* emphasize the book itself as the body waking up through the agency of being read:

> My young mother, her face narrow
> and dark with unresolved wishes
> under a hatbrim of the twenties,
> stood by my middleaged bed.
>
> Still as a child pretending sleep
> to a grownup watchful or calling,
> I lay in the a corner of my dream
> staring at the mole above her lip.
>
> Familiar mole! but that girlish look
> as if I had nothing to give her—
> Eyes blue—brim dark—
> calling me from sleep after decades.

(53)

This is a poetry with faith in poetry as an enactment of music, or perhaps I should say an *embodiment* of music. The mother's mole is rendered tenderly through the exclamation point, a punctuation mark Cooper loved, using it often to score shifts in register. (I count eighteen of them in the first twenty poems of Section 1: "Puritanical signature!" "No more elegies!") Here, it emphasizes the mind's dreamy disjuncture. Cooper's unassailable craft expresses the liminal state of sleep through the first stanzas' lyric regularity, finally offset by the wakeful disruptions of the last stanza, making the poem and its message seemingly fated: *calling me from sleep.*

In the essay at the center of *Maps & Windows,* Cooper asks if her narrative of the buried book is a political story, "having to do with how hard it is for a woman to *feel* the freedom that would let her develop as a writer, even when she has it? Is it a tale of personal neurosis? Or is it simply the history of one individual woman. . . ."[2] Cooper was seventeen when Pearl Harbor was attacked and a senior in college when atomic bombs were dropped on Hiroshima and Nagasaki. She studied meteorology and other sciences at college, then switched to languages. When World War II ended, she was at home with her family in Princeton as returning G.I.s flooded the campus. Marriage was her anticipated future.

The essay, "Nothing Has Been Used in the Manufacture of This Poetry That Could Have Been Used in the Manufacture of Bread," is an autobiography of her writing life set within a political context of destructive binary forces: marriage or writing, love or honesty. If a younger audience is impatient with these binary disquisitions from the 1940s and '50s . . . the project itself embodies the corrosiveness of their historical reality.

The buried book, "Mercator's World," was named for the sixteenth-century Flemish cartographer whose navigational maps of the world skewed geographical relationships due to the disjuncture between three-dimensional space and its representation on a flat surface. In the essay preceding "Mercator's World," Cooper is astute about her younger self's dilemma. She craved the radical insights she perceived to be poetry's *raison d'être,* but she feared those insights were destructive to the delicate relationships between men and women.[3] She writes, "Somehow, I was trying, in imagination, to revive some perfect model of the trap I had to spring."[4] Here, from the buried book is the opening stanza of "The Urge to Tell the Truth," written in 1949 when the poet was twenty-five years old: "The urge to tell the truth / Strips sensuality / Like bark stripped from a tree."[5] And the remarkable first stanza of "Twins," from 1949–1951: "You ask for love but what you want is healing. / Selfishly, understandably. You pray / For marriage as another man might pray / For sleep after surgery. . . ."[6]

Though it was written over a thirty-year span, there is a consistency of presence and intellect throughout *Maps & Windows* . . . and the subject of a woman's sexuality is implicit in all: "Sex floated like a moon / over the composition. . . ."[7] Sexuality, indivisible from a woman's body, which may be buried or erased. In the poems of "Mercator's World," the problem of the body becomes the problem of the social derogation of female sexual presence: "For what do you see when I / Come to you? Isn't it woman, / Passion, a pair of eyes, the ground / To prove old sex and sorrows on?"[8]

Is it anger that buried her book?

It is the work of the prose section to speak directly about the warped social expectations and literary atmosphere she confronted. She quotes the first line of her teacher John Berryman's "Dream Song 187" early in her essay: "Them lady poets must not marry." Here is his whole, revealing first stanza: "Them lady poets must not marry, pal. / Miss Dickinson—fancy in Amherst bedding her. / Fancy a lark with Sappho, / a tumble in the bushes with Miss Moore, / a spoon with Emily, while Charlotte glare. / Miss Bishop's too noble-O. . . ."[9]

Berryman was also a product of this time, and in 1948, Cooper recorded a conversation with him that became "poem without capital letters," from the buried book: "john berryman asked me to write a poem about roosters. / elizabeth bishop, he said, once wrote a poem about roosters. / *do your poems use capital letters*? he asked. *like god*? / i said. *god no*, he said, *like princeton*! I said, / *god preserve me if I ever write a poem about princeton*! and I thought / o john berryman, what has brought me into this company of poets / where the masculine thing to do is use capital letters . . . ?"[10] When she asks herself what caused her to bury her book, she demurs. Was it her own coercive perfectionism?[11] Or was it that she was not ready for what the poems knew?

Jane Cooper was my faculty advisor at Sarah Lawrence College during my sophomore year, filling in for Grace Paley who was on leave. Only now have I realized that my conversations with Jane occurred during the year *Maps & Windows* appeared. Jane sat—do I remember correctly?—on a hard wood chair while I pooled into a padded sofa. She was frail and tall. Secretly, I wanted a role model like Grace—more overtly sexy, messy and dramatically political. I was not a student of creative writing, and Jane's nuanced artistry was largely unknown to me; but we shared an interest in looking at nature closely, and we talked about my first trip back to Italy, my birth country. Jane had been too sick when visiting Italy to enjoy it, which led to her tactful description of her illness and its required routines. To the nineteen-year-old-girl-I-was, her life seemed sadly proscribed.

The gift of *Maps & Windows* has grown for me over time and speaks to me now about adulthood: choices, other free beings, the voice as an embodiment of action. Stephen Burt has written brilliantly that "a poem can stand in for, or create an alternative to, a human face and a human body . . . we might enjoy reading and writing poetry for many reasons but we feel that we need figuration, need something unavailable in the literal world."[12] *Maps & Windows*—generated by the difficulties of making a life as an artist, and the final, storied nurture of a body of work—figuratively gives life to the *woman's* body. The poem "Waiting" was a threshold not only to the poet's greater self-possession, but to a growing honesty about the female body itself—honesty, which I have benefited from along with the rest of my generation of writers. "My body knows it will never bear children. / What can I say to my body now, / this used violin?"[13]

Cooper's friend Adrienne Rich would write *Of Woman Born: Motherhood as Experience and Institution* a few years after "Waiting," incubating a wider cultural dialogue about the politics of motherhood. Articulation of childlessness—"Old body, old friend, / why are you so unforgiving?"— was, and still is, radical—body-bear-body-box-box. Awakening is the question "Suppose you are an empty box?" and its answer: "Let compassion breathe in and out of you / filling you with poems." A book is also a box—but as we read, it is a transformative experience in which, finally, the whole woman is permitted to speak.

Forty years since *Maps & Windows* first appeared, there is a candor about sexuality in our country that was almost unimaginable in the early '70s. The changes that the sexual revolution made in our society—some still aspirational, many still contested—are our inheritance. Jane Cooper's artistry and act of recovery was part of this conversation. *Maps & Windows* opened a way, not just for her but for my generation, and the next. For many human beings around the globe, right now, the loneliness explored in *Maps & Windows* is still unfolding, and the path toward self-possession is neither safe nor certain. Every time and place renegotiates an understanding of what is possible, and each person must decide for herself. If she is lucky and she perseveres, she may "live in the future / like a survivor! / Not the first step up the beach / but the second / then the third. . . ."[14] *Thank you, Jane.*

Notes

1. Jane Cooper, *Maps & Windows* (New York: Macmillan, 1974), 3.
2. Ibid., 52.
3. Ibid., 50.
4. Ibid., 42.
5. Ibid., 65.
6. Ibid., 67.
7. Ibid., 22.
8. Ibid., 64
9. John Berryman, *The Dream Songs* (New York: Farrar, Straus, and Giroux, 2007), 206.
10. Jane Cooper, *Maps & Windows*, 63.
11. Ibid., 49.
12. Stephen Burt, "The Body of the Poem: On Transgender Poetry," *Los Angeles Review of Books*, November 17, 2013.
13. Jane Cooper, *Maps & Windows*, 27.
14. Jane Cooper, *The Flashboat: Poems Collected and Reclaimed* (New York: Norton, 2000), 157.

PHILIP LEVINE

Endurance

HOLDING OUT

Letters come, the phone rings, you sit by your window
balancing yourself like a last glass of water.

All over the city the hospitals are crammed with wounded.
Divorce, like marriage, requires two adversaries.

But what is left now is not to exaggerate:
your grief, his grief—these serious possessions.

(131)

Why does this simple poem possess so much power, why does the
initial reading of it ask for another reading and still another? Let me
attempt some answers by suggesting that its power resides both in
the spoken and the unspoken, and that the conversation the poem
enacts is so dramatic that it forces itself to end because it has over-
whelmed the consciousness at the center. The letters which arrive,
the telephone calls—answered or not—haven't the authority to
break in on this treasured, though painful, dialogue. Notice that
each couplet possesses a startling remark: in the first stanza, it is the
difficult balancing act. Consider the alternative, the loss of balancing
oneself like a glass of water, not an ordinary glass of water but a pre-
cious final one: the result is spillage, not merely of water but of an
internal balance that most certainly will result in tears or worse,
possibly temporary madness.

The focus abruptly shifts in the second stanza to the city that lies
outside the window and insists on its presence. Although the private
drama is overwhelmed, perhaps even belittled—in a public
sense—by the hospitals crammed with those with physical
wounds—and possibly mental ones as well—the personal takes pre-
cedence over the pain of the larger world. Divorce, we know, takes

79

two adversaries, but marriage? In the wisdom of the poem, yes, marriage also.

The third stanza provides us with the lesson: the listener—and let me suggest here that the listener is the speaker trying her best to behave with the composure and dignity she prefers—is told not to make more of her crisis than it merits, especially because it brings with it two helpings of extraordinary grief, his and yours. These are not trivial items: they are "serious possessions." In the precise and restrained use of language under enormous emotional pressure, Jane Cooper's little poem reminds one of the exactitude and power of ancient Chinese poetry, and reminds me especially of another six-line poem, this by Wu Han, another poem of grief from lost love.

GONE

The sound of her silk skirt has stopped.
On the marble pavement dust grows.
Her empty room is cold and still.
Fallen leaves are piled against the doors.
Longing for that lovely lady
How can I bring my aching heart to rest?

Translated by Arthur Waley

In the Chinese poem, there is a strong suggestion that the loss is through death; whether or not this is preferable to loss through estrangement I can't say. In both poems, the balance of the spoken and unspoken adds to both the mystery and the tension; both are about "holding out," that is surviving traumatic loss and still living within one's own sense of decorum. It is interesting to note that when Ezra Pound translated this poem—it's in *Personae*, his collection of 1912—he fudged on the final line. The good Imagist Ezra wrote, "A wet leaf that clings to the threshold," a sense totally absent from the four other translations I consulted. Was he afraid of "my aching heart"? He was writing before country western music seized international attention and would make the line sound worse than it is. Jane Cooper, however, is unafraid to call grief by its name, and indeed, in her short and brave poem is unafraid of anything except tactlessness. She treats her reader with the same respect she would ask of all poetry; she does so continually, and that is why her poetry will survive.

RACHEL HADAS

An Ecstasy of Space

Scaffolding, the title of Jane Cooper's *New and Selected Poems,* suggests a support system, a work in constant progress (scaffolding put up while repairs are made), and also a skeletal, stripped-down intensity—all apt figures for this poet's quest for clarity and impulse toward self-revision. Adrienne Rich refers on the back cover of *Scaffolding* to Copper's "continuing inner growth," and Cooper herself, in her foreword, speaks of "the continuous journey the work has been for me all along." Cooper's oeuvre indeed refuses to stand still, which may be one reason critics have tended to detour around it. Nevertheless, the image of scaffolding is more evocative than that of a journey when one considers Cooper's career. It's as if the inner growth Rich mentions is achieved by continually peeling away layer after layer; what once was essential now seems superfluous, and is calmly or exuberantly discarded to make room for the new.

What's the new like? The spareness of Cooper's recent work cuts both ways:

> For the last few years, particularly, we have all lived with the threat of nuclear holocaust. I want just to suggest it through images of all-consuming light, rooms with only a few sticks left in them, and a stripped-down landscape that is both the joyous, essential condition of truth telling and an almost unbearable vision of the future.
>
> (from the Foreword)

So the bright, bare room is both a joyful vision and a frightful glimpse of a bleak wasteland. Once the scaffolding is finally dismantled, we will have arrived at both heaven and hell.

One way to look at Cooper's work as *Scaffolding* presents it is to chart her progress toward that dangerous bright edge. We can note what has happened to the lineation, the prosody, even the punctuation between a poem from *"Mercator's World"* (1947–51) and one from *The Flashboat* (1975–83).

Head first, face down, into Mercator's world
Like an ungainly rocket the child comes,
Driving dead-reckoned outward through a channel
Where nine months back breath was determined
By love, leaving his watery pen
—That concrete womb with its round concrete walls
Which he could make a globe of all his own—
For flatter, dryer enemies, for home.

                              (from "For a Boy Born in Wartime")

The future weighs down on me
just like a wall of light!

All these years
I've lived by necessity.
Now the world shines
like an empty room
clean all the way to the rafters.
. . . .
To live in the future
like a survivor!
Not the first step up the beach
but the second
then the third

—never forgetting
the wingprint of the mountain
over the fragile human settlement—

                                        ("The Blue Anchor")

The packed pentameter lines of "For a Boy" tend to split in "The
Blue Anchor" into pairs of shorter lines with two or three stresses
apiece, gaining greater speed as the syntactical texture is thinned
out. The eight quoted lines of "For a Boy" are less than a complete
sentence; "Blue Anchor" is almost breathlessly simple by contrast.
Alliteration and assonance foster teeming connections within al-
most every line of "For a Boy" but are sparse in "Anchor," true to
the poetics of the empty room. "For a Boy" is altogether more clot-
ted, ponderous, and rich to read; one could liken the very different
beauty of "The Blue Anchor" to that paradoxical wall of light, both
shining and disembodied.

But careful chronological tracing seems the wrong tactic when we encounter a single (and crucial) poem, "All These Dreams," which is dated 1967–83. How do you disentangle the styles on a palimpsest? And it's also discouraging to an historical approach that Cooper has chosen to put her memorable 1974 essay, "Nothing Has Been Used in the Manufacture of This Poetry That Could Have Been Used in the Manufacture of Bread," between "*Mercator's World*" and "*The Weather of Six Mornings*"—that is, between groups of poems dated respectively 1947–51 and 1954–65. Why, for that matter, include an essay at all in a selected poems collection? "Nothing Has Been Used" is less an aesthetic manifesto (if it were, surely it would have been placed first in the collection) than an invaluable guide to Cooper's fluid but distinctive sensibility and style. The essay gives us an extended hearing of a voice that is necessarily curtailed in Cooper's usually short poems. Honest, self-critical, vehement without bravado, that voice comes through, for example, when Cooper remembers that

> during one of my interviews [at Sarah Lawrence] I was asked, "And why do you think you can teach poetry?" and I answered, "Because it's the one place where I'd as soon take my own word as anybody else's," though I went on to say that that didn't mean I thought I was always right!

Too shifting to be summarized without distortion, the argument of "Nothing Has Been Used" is faithful to the growth and change that are Cooper's themes. Like Emerson, Cooper is hard to paraphrase, but inspiring to read, and—as she leaps from autobiographical incident to piercing aphorism—tempting to quote from. Some of the comments about poetry in "Nothing Has Been Used" are worth pondering for any lover of poetry.

> For what poetry must do is alert us to a truth, and it must be necessary; once it exists, we realize how much we needed exactly this.

> A poem uses everything we know, the surprising things we notice, whatever we can't solve that keeps on growing, but it has to reach beyond autobiography even to stay on the page. Autobiography is not true enough . . . .

"I have a very old-fashioned idea of what poetry should do. It is the soul's history and whatever troubles the soul is fit material for poetry."

T. S. Eliot long ago pointed out that when poets make general statements about poetry, it is their own work they have in mind. Any reader of these passages can infer that Cooper has a lofty yet grounded notion of the nature and mission of poetry, as derived from facts but needing to transcend them. Despite a protean multiplicity of styles and indeed of subjects ("whatever troubles the soul is fit material"), poetry is marked for her by its high seriousness, its power and obligation to tell the truth.

A problematic part of that truth, for Cooper, is her earlier work. The poems from the 1940s and 1950s may seem to her insufficiently genuine, too influenced by other (and largely male) poets; yet she concludes "Nothing Has Been Used" by saying she has learned to accept those poems "as part of whatever I now am . . . . For if my poems have always been about survival—and I believe they have been—then survival too keeps revealing itself as an art of the unexpected."

I love the way that sentence twists in one's hands, refusing to end until it has completed its thought in an unexpected way. And the thought, like the entire essay, is complicated. To put it crudely, Cooper is both endorsing and condemning her early work. Her tone seems generous; yet a reader can easily be swayed into agreeing with what is perhaps implied: that the more recent poems are in some way more valuable than the early work. (Or *is* that implied? Cooper's delicacy of tone leaves us room to wonder.)

It is characteristic of Cooper that she relegates a recurrent theme of her work to a subordinate clause. The poems may indeed be about survival. The question, though, is less what Cooper writes about than how she writes. Has her style been crucially changed by the progressive simplifying we can discern between the full lines and complex syntax of "For a Boy Born in Wartime" and the almost hectic immediacy, and great emphasis on the self, that we see in "The Blue Anchor"?

My answer would be that a family resemblance is discernible between most of the poems in *Scaffolding*, and that the shared features include concision and exactness; careful attention to details both of appearance and of mood; a strong sense of the line; and finally, a rejection of facile endings. These are not easy qualities to describe in literary terms. Grace Paley has well expressed what many of Cooper's admirers must feel: "This is a beautiful and stubborn book of poems. The poems say only what they mean." Is this a negative virtue? It's true that Cooper can be praised in negative terms: she avoids sloppiness, sentimentality, and—perhaps most unusual for a poet of her generation—obscurity. Following her own precept that poetry must go beyond autobiography, she speaks of large matters without sacrificing personal experience or an intimate voice.

In fact, Cooper's voice may be the most distinctive feature of her work. It reminds me of "the low tones that decide" (Emerson's phrase in "Uriel"), and also of the two aunts in *Swann's Way*, helplessly well-bred and subtle, who thank M. Swann for his gift of wine in such discreetly veiled terms that no one but their family understands them. Not that Cooper is cryptic; it's just that she's incapable of raising her voice or putting things coarsely, whether she's writing in the forties about World War II or in the seventies about a dream of communality. Words such as "delicate" and "nice" have become terribly suspect: Adrienne Rich has written (and Cooper cites her) of the pressures on women writers of their generation to be "nice." As for "delicate," that adjective was applied to the present writer in a recent magazine article, evoking derision from all kinds of friends and acquaintances. Some other word must be found to convey the finely wrought and modulated character of Cooper's work from first to last, and her unremittingly ardent set of standards for both the style and the substance of her poetry.

An early poem that Cooper includes in *Scaffolding*, "Long View from the Suburbs," is a dramatic monologue in which Cooper attempts to "invent how it might feel to be the old Maud Gonne, whose extraordinary photographs had appeared in *Life* magazine" (from "Nothing Has Been Used"). So much for the poem's provenance; as for its style, Cooper says that "the rhetoric remains heavy (that need to write long lines, to have a battery of sound-effects at my command—like a man?)." She fails to do justice here to the originality and, yes, delicacy of her own effects. Yeats may have contributed something in the poem's conception, and Auden, surely, to phrases like "A streetlight yielded to the sensual air." But the searchingly quiet mode of the poem is already Cooper's alone:

Once for instance
He begged to meet me under an oak
Outside the city after five o'clock.
It was early April. I waited there
Until in the distance
A streetlight yielded to the sensual air.

Then I walked home again. The next day
He was touchy and elated
Because of a new poem which he said
Marked some advance—perhaps that "honest" style
Which prostitutes our memories.
He gave it to me. I said nothing at all

Being weary. It had happened so often.
He was always deluding himself
Complaining (honestly) that I spurned his gifts.
Shall I tell you what gifts are? Although I said
Nothing at the time
I still remember evenings when I learned

The tricks of style. . . .

The poem hovers between the figure of Gonne and a probable ac-
cumulation of personal experiences as nimbly as its sentences cross
stanzas. With a charming authority the tone glides between rueful
amusement, amused anger, and weary exasperation at male grandi-
osity and importunate enthusiasms. Note the eloquent sigh ("it had
happened so often") and the barbed parenthetical "honestly." No
wonder many poets sacrifice such subtleties for more unmixed rhe-
torical effects; for reading "Long View," we can neither wholly sym-
pathize with nor wholly condemn the wry and ghostly resonance
of a speaking voice that both is and is not a persona. Cooper moves
beyond biography here. We don't need to know about Maud Gonne
to savor the subtleties and ironies—and the aside (the low voice
dropping still lower?) about that "honest" style that prostitutes our
memories is surely a reflection of Cooper's own feeling about the
kind of desperately autobiographical poetry, exemplified by Lowell
and Berryman, that was coming into vogue around the time "Long
View" was written.

    If the "I" in "Long View" both is and isn't a persona, there is no
"I" at all in "For a Boy Born in Wartime." Cooper moves closer, as

the years pass, to some center from which that skinny pronoun can authoritatively issue; yet her use of the first person is mostly exploratory, tentative, low-key, until the pivotal "All These Dreams" (dated 1967–83). Even that poem, with its unusual aposiopesis and exclamations, is full of questions.

> Where have I escaped from? What have I escaped to?
> Why has my child no father?
> I must be halfway up the circular stair.
> To shape my own—
>   Friends! I hold out my hands
> as all that light pours down, it is pouring down.

In very general terms, the shift of emphasis in Cooper's work is from more public poems (of war) to more private poems (of love, family, dreams, work). Yet one must immediately qualify. The "public" poems were inward in their questing, and the "private" poems open out to speak to concerns as far-flung as nuclear holocaust, or what it means to be a woman, or—in the latest poem here, "Threads,"—what it felt like to be Rosa Luxemburg in prison. Indeed, in "Threads," Cooper presents Luxemburg in a way that forces us to revise any pat notion of this woman as a merely political figure:

> We live in the painfulest moment of evolution,
> the very chapter of change, and you have to ask,
> *What is the meaning of it all?* Listen,
> one day I found a beetle stunned on its back,
> its legs gnawed to stumps by ants; another day
> I clambered to free a peacock butterfly
> battering half dead inside our bathroom pane.
> Locked up myself after six, I lean on the sill.
> The sky's like iron, a heavy rain falls, the nightingale
> sings in the sycamore as if possessed.

Imprisoned for her radical beliefs and opposition to World War I, Luxemburg tries to shed the weight of despair by passionately studying nature, especially birds and geology and insect life. But she cannot help seeing—and mourning—the painful struggles of historical change that have their deadly counterpart in the laws of evolution. Her intervention to save the peacock butterfly comes too late.

But just as Cooper's controlled tone is a pretty dependable constant, so we come to count on the images that surface throughout *Scaffolding*, images that help to shape the soul's troubles into art. One image is clearly signaled by the title of the 1970–83 poems but can also be seen elsewhere: dispossessions. Cooper is working her way toward what, as we've seen, she calls "rooms with only a few sticks left in them . . . a stripped down landscape." We see the inner and outer bareness in the programmatic "All These Dreams":

> All these dreams, this obsession with bare boards:
> scaffolding, with only a few objects
> in an ecstasy of space, where through the windows
> the scent of pines can blow in . . .
> . . . .
> O serenity
> that can live without chairs . . .

It took many readings for me to connect this passage with Thoreau's ecstatically ascetic mysticism, with Andrew Marvell's withdrawing mind in "The Garden," and perhaps also with some of George Herbert's plainly furnished rooms. But "All These Dreams" doesn't feel literary in the way that "Long View" or "For a Boy Born in Wartime" evidently came to feel to Cooper; it is a disembodied vision that is also a joyful *cri de coeur*, as familiar and strange as the dream state it evokes.

Less elated than the vision in "All These Dreams" is this fuller account of the same impulse toward spring-cleaning in "Souvenirs," the second poem in the splendid three-poem title sequence of "*Dispossessions*." I quote "Souvenirs" in full:

> Anyway we are always waking
> in bedrooms of the dead, smelling
> musk of their winter jackets, tracking
> prints of their heels across our blurred carpets.
>
> So why hang onto a particular postcard?
> If a child's lock of hair brings back
> the look of that child, shall I
> nevertheless not let it blow away?
>
> Houses, houses, we lodge in such husks!
> inhabit such promises, seeking the unborn

in a worn-out photograph, hoping to break free
even of our violent and faithful lives.

Every detail of these expert lines seems to throw poetic light on a
domestic dilemma, and vice versa. (The muse as pack rat or house-
cleaner; as the superego from whom we hope "to break free," or the
magical link with the past?) As its title indicates, "Souvenirs" is no
mere list of totems but concerns the act of remembering; yet part
of the poem's persuasiveness surely derives from the reader's cer-
tainty that these carpets, jackets, locks of hair, and postcards are real,
that Cooper is writing from abundance, not decorating emptiness
with synthetic images.

The emblem of the house full of relics, that postcard especially
memorable, reminds me of similar concerns in the work of two of
Cooper's contemporaries, Adrienne Rich and James Merrill, whose
different approaches to divesting themselves of the weight of the
past are discussed in the late David Kalstone's illuminating book
Five Temperaments. Rich's "Meditation for a Savage Child," writes
Kalstone, juxtaposes "indignation with a residual attraction to fa-
miliar objects and the habit of cherishing." In Merrill's "The Friend
of the Fourth Decade," the past is epitomized (as for Cooper in
"Souvenirs") by postcards, but throwing them out—or as the friend
suggests, rinsing the ink off—doesn't work: "the memories they
stirred did not elude me." Ruefully, Merrill acknowledges the
power of what Cooper calls worn-out photographs:

I put my postcards back upon the shelf.
Certain things die only with oneself.

One wishes Cooper had found a place among Kalstone's tempera-
ments.

The voice in "Souvenirs" is vehement but not angry. "So why
hang onto a particular postcard?" sounds to me like an honest ques-
tion, not a rhetorical posture; and "shall I / nevertheless not let it
blow away?" is similarly a thought, not—or not yet—a dismissal.
The same rapt, feeling-its-ways intuition toward a desired space
makes itself felt in "Rent," from the 1975–83 group *The Flashboat*:

I don't want your rent, I want
a radiance of attention
like the candle's flame when we eat,

I mean a kind of awe
attending the spaces between us—
Not a roof but a field of stars.

Notice the poem's rapid zoom from the couple at the candlelit table
to the "field of stars"—a change of weather indeed, and scale, and
tone, and light.

Such an outdoor space is also the scene of "Praise." The decks
have been cleared, and work/play is in progress, beyond the norm:

Between five and fifty
most people construct a little lifetime:
they fall in love, make kids, they suffer
and pitch the usual tents of understanding.
But I have built a few unexpected bridges.
Out of inert stone, with its longing to embrace inert stone,
I have sent a few vaults into stainless air.
Is this enough—when I love our poor sister earth?
Sister earth, I kneel and ask pardon.
A clod of turf is no less than inert stone.
Nothing is enough!
In this field set free for our play
who could have foretold
I would live to write at fifty?

"Who could have foretold I would set the field free?" might be
another way of putting it. The poem is a kind of psalm to (re)cre-
ation; mere dispossession has yielded both to a more sublime blank-
ness and to a different kind of construction—a creation not of do-
mestic interiors or of kids, but of architecture—more scaffolding! I
myself feel more at home with the Cooper of "Souvenirs," but the
elation in *The Flashboat* comes from somewhere; it feels honest and
earned.

Companion to the successive strippings in Cooper's work is an
image harder to describe. It might be called recognition, or self-
scrutiny, or looking into a mirror, or meeting someone else's
eyes—or meeting one's own. The self, after all, cannot be thrown
away like a "particular postcard" or a lock of hair; it changes, and we
can keep track of the changes by focusing from time to time on the
latest manifestation of what we are. As early as "For a Boy Born in
Wartime," Cooper refers to "the concrete / Unmalleable mirror

world we live in." The mirror slowly clears as the poems continue, but it takes a long time to be able to see oneself.[1]

> Feelings aside I never know my face;
> I comb my hair and what I see is timeless,
> Not a face at all but (besides the hair)
> Lips and a pair of eyes, two hands, a body
> Pale as a fish imprisoned in the mirror.
>
> (from "The Knowledge That Comes
Through Experience")

That fish-pale body is unsettlingly reminiscent of Sylvia Plath's image of a woman looking in a mirror and seeing an old woman rise in it "like a terrible fish," though as we might expect, Cooper is more controlled in her distaste for what she sees.

One solution to the problem of appearances, in *The Weather of Six Mornings,* is to address oneself as another. Indeed, the self presented by an old photograph (which has evidently not yet been discarded) *is* another. "Leaving Water Hyacinths" (subtitled "from an old photograph") begins "I see you, child, standing above the river" and moves, at the start of each successive stanza, to a closer identification of speaker with image: "I know—because you become me" and finally "I know—because you contain me."

In two remarkable poems—apparently about her mother but actually, I think, about the double layering of selves (younger and older mother; younger and older daughter)—Cooper is true to the difficulty not only of making images of ourselves, but of reconstructing the appearances even of those we love:

> Why can I never when I think about it
> See your face tender under the tasseled light
> Above a book held in your stubby fingers?
> Or catch your tumbling gamecock angers?
> Or—as a child once, feverish by night—
> Wake to your sleepless, profiled granite?
>
> But I must reconstruct you, feature by feature:
> Your sailor's gaze, a visionary blue,
> Not stay-at-home but wistful northern eyes;
> And the nose Gothic, oversized,
> Delicately groined to the eyesockets' shadow,
> Proud as a precipice above laughter.

A curious cubism supplies us with more visual details than we can well assimilate; the reconstruction is no more "realistic" than a Picasso portrait, and, yet (or therefore), communicates powerfully what struggles to find a niche in memory. These lines, which splendidly render back what the speaker says she can't see, are from a poem entitled "For My Mother in Her First Illness, from a Window Overlooking Notre Dame"; yet at the poem's close, it is the daughter who is ill: "Alone and sick, lying in a foreign house, / I try to read. Which one of us is absent?"

A similar pentimento gives an uncanny doubleness to "My Young Mother," quoted here in full:

My young mother, her face narrow
and dark with unresolved wishes
under a hatbrim of the twenties,
stood by my middleaged bed.

Still as a child pretending to sleep
to a grownup watchful or calling,
I lay in a corner of my dream
starting at the mole above her lip.

Familiar mole! but that girlish look
as if I had nothing to give her—
Eyes blue—brim dark—
calling me from sleep after decades.

Mother and daughter, past and present: The successive embodiments merge with a fluency reflected in Cooper's supple and sparing use of the first person. A poem about her mother, for example, twists into one about her, rather as a letter that begins by politely eschewing the writer's concerns manages gracefully to arrive at some personal news. Survival, Cooper has said, keeps revealing itself an art of the unexpected; the unexpectedness of some of Cooper's shifts of emphasis surely has the spryness and resilience necessary for survival.

Cooper is able to invest poems that almost or completely suppress the first person with a searching intimacy that constitutes a kind of mirroring at a remove. "Waiting" and "A Circle, a Square, a Triangle and a Ripple of Water," neighboring poems from "*Dispossessions,*" look at, and into, not only the eyes but the entire body, both in itself and, especially in "A Circle," in relation to others.

My body knows it will never bear children.
What can I say to my body now,
this used violin?
Every night it cries out strenuously
from its secret cave.

(from "Waiting")

Seemingly untouched she
was the stone at the center of
the pool whose circles
shuddered off around her.

(from "A Circle")

It wouldn't be hard to rewrite this pair of passages so that "Waiting" was in the third person and "A Circle" in the first person, so precise is Cooper's intimacy, and so passionate her observation.

At about the point in Cooper's work where she reaches the ecstasies of empty space, the images of self-searching stop. The overlay of one's parents is, by middle age, a thing of the past—still there, no doubt, but no longer news. And a new kind of mirror can be found in the gaze of like-minded companions and other variants of reflection. In "All These Dreams," there is no mirror—after all there are no rooms, and presumably no walls—but "light poured down through the roof on a circular stair / made of glass." And at the poem's close, which I quoted earlier but must return to, Cooper interrupts herself in the midst of shaping . . . what?

I must be halfway up the circular stair.
To shape my own—

My own image? self? work? Her word does double duty as the object of "to shape" and as a glad apostrophe: "Friends!"

That circular stair is a good emblem for Cooper's work. It may recall Yeats's winding stair, but it has its own radiance; and the poet is halfway up it, not in a dark wood but in a group of friends, laughing. The most rewarding thing about *Scaffolding* is the way Cooper's scrupulous and profoundly serious art moves toward joy.

Note

1. A poem entitled "In a Room with Picassos" addresses a similar problem of appearances:

Draw as you will there are no images
Which exactly reproduce this state of mind!

And, from "The Door" (also from this early group): "For what do you see when I / Come to you . . . What do you see?"

JEAN VALENTINE

Dreamwords

THE FLASHBOAT

I

A high deck. Blue skies overhead. White distance.
The wind on my tongue. A day of days. From the shore a
    churchbell clangs.
Below me the grinding of floes: tiny families huddled together
earth-colored. Let me explain, the ice is cracking free.
They were cut off unawares. From the shore a churchbell clangs.
When the ice breaks up it is spring. No
comfort, no comfort.

2

And here is that part of my dream I would like to forget. The purser
is at his desk, he is leaning toward me out of his seat, he is my tor-
turer who assumes we think alike. Again and again he questions me
as to which national boundaries I plan to cross. *Are you a political
activist? No, I'm a teacher.* But already the villagers have been swept
out to sea. We are cruising north of the Arctic Circle. Without haste
he locks my passport away in his breast pocket. Was I wrong to de-
clare myself innocent?

3

(I did not protest. I spoke nothing but the truth. I never spoke of
that girl who kneeled by her skyscraper window, falling without a
sound through the New York City night.)

4

Now it's our turn. Three A.M.
and the Queen Mary is sinking.
All is bustle—but in grays. Red lanterns crawl here and there.
The crew makes ready the boats. One near me, broad but shallow,

95

looks safe, women are urged, the captain will be in charge.
Far down now: a trough. A smaller dory rocks
in and out of our lights; black fists grip the oars.
Room only for six—we will
all need to row.
For a moment I hesitate, worrying about my defective blood.
A rope ladder drops over. My voice with its crunch of bone
wakes me: *I choose*
the flashboat!

             work,

                    the starry waters

                              (143–44)

I love "The Flashboat"—you know dreamwords when you hear them!—for its beauty and its courage. In those ways, it seems to me to be a signature poem of Jane Cooper's. I love the beauty and the courage of its choice: I imagine it as a continuing choice, with continuing dream- and poem-light shining on it, over many years: "*I choose / the flashboat!*"

Sometimes I think of Jane Cooper and Eleanor Ross Taylor together, in a few ways: they were both Southern, very close in age, and both highly educated, by institutions and by their own selves. Both have/had the impression—as Elizabeth Bishop did, too—that they hadn't written much. But what is "much"? I feel what those women wrote and published (so far!) is a fullness. Perhaps our ideas of measurement are changing. And both Cooper and Taylor were going to collide, Cooper more, with politics: class, money, convention, race, inner survival.

People say, about others usually, "She fell far from the tree." Often, I'd say, it's not falling but flying; and then a long (if you're lucky) triathlon.

In 1: The first two lines are high-class, with a pleasing aspect:

A high deck. Blue skies overhead. White distance.
The wind on my tongue. A day of days. From the shore a
    churchbell clangs.

But a hint of change: "white distance." "clangs." Then:

Below me the grinding of floes: tiny families huddled together
earth-colored. Let me explain, the ice is cracking free.
They were cut off unawares. From the shore a churchbell clangs.

Again, the churchbell. And the distance: "tiny" families. "Earth-colored." What color is that? But the ice is cracking "free."

In the next two lines:

When the ice breaks up it is spring. No
comfort, no comfort.

For a minute, things seem more cheerful; but no. There is a world of turn in those seven lines, reflected in their leisurely seven or six beats that shift down to four, then two; a motion that will be repeated in the poem's fourth section—a motion towards seriousness.

In 2: ". . . I would like to forget."

And indeed, here the dream is at its most rational, in prose; perhaps it is half-forgotten or censored. It seems the speaker here is arguing half with others and half with herself.

3: Prose again: a parenthetical swerve, the nothing-but-the-truth lie.

"That girl" whom the poet, or at any rate the dream, remembers.

4: "Now it's our turn."

(After that girl's turn?)

All is bustle—but in grays. Red lanterns crawl here and there.
The crew makes ready the boats. One near me, broad but shallow,
looks safe, women are urged, the captain will be in charge.
Far down now: a trough. A smaller dory rocks
in and out of our lights; black fists grip the oars.

"Fists"—land blows; signal protest, anger, strength, danger. And then "My voice with its crunch of bone" takes me back to "the grinding of floes" and "the ice is cracking free":

For a moment I hesitate, worrying about my defective blood.
A rope ladder drops over. My voice with its crunch of bone
wakes me: *I choose*
the flashboat!
                work,
                        the starry waters

I last saw Jane Cooper a few weeks before she died; she was very thin, and her eyes were welcoming. She asked me about my poetry, and I said I was meeting now and then with some poets she knew, to share our work. She said, "I'd like to be there with you, ahead of time!"

By and by, she said it was time for her to go to her reading group, a group of some of her best friends in the retirement community. "What are you reading?" I asked. A huge smile: "Dante's *Inferno.*" "Oh Jane. Couldn't it at least be *Purgatorio?*" Another huge, rather affectionately mocking smile: "No—we have to go in the proper order."

2008

THOMAS LUX

The Fragile Human Settlement

THE BLUE ANCHOR

The future weighs down on me
just like a wall of light!

All these years
I've lived by necessity.
Now the world shines
like an empty room
clean all the way to the rafters.

The room might be waiting for its first tenants—
a bed, a chair, my old typewriter.

Or it might be Van Gogh's room
at Arles:
so neat, while his eyes grazed among phosphorus.
A blue anchor.

To live in the future
like a survivor!
Not the first step up the beach
but the second
then the third

—never forgetting
the wingprint of the mountain
over the fragile human settlement—

(157)

I have always loved this poem by Jane Cooper.

Sure, it begins with a fairly familiar word coupling, future/
weighs, but then—because she knows it's fairly familiar—she gives
it new resonance by comparing it to a wall (something that blocks
us rather than weighing down on us) of light. Light: we can walk
through that; it has no weight. There are contradictory notions at

work here, but the future is in the affirmative. I can't recall a more appropriate, earned, and courageous exclamation point in contemporary American poetry!

The second stanza continues this affirmation. The speaker has lived many years "by necessity": bare bones, paycheck to paycheck, doing the necessary work, the appointed tasks? The next simile parallels the simile in the first stanza, an overwhelmingly large thing, the world, compared to a room "clean all the way to the rafters." That's a *very* clean room! A room full of hope.

This room doesn't need much, only what's necessary: a bed ("I have sleep to do / I have work to dream"[1]), a chair, the speaker's old typewriter. The use of the provisional ("might be") is smart here, is very deliberate. It would seem immodest since it might also be Van Gogh's room at Arles (we've all seen the paintings). This turn to Van Gogh provides for me a stunning and accurate metaphor for the genius of his vision and its execution: "his eyes grazed among phosphorus." "Grazed" is a brilliant verb here with its cows and bucolic connotations, and then it turns, with the beautiful logic of illogic, to a tasty, tasty word, "phosphorus," a yellowish wax-like chemical that glows in the dark. It is also used as a fertilizer and, I believe, as a component in certain explosives. *All* of the connotations are right! We never have to read a line of art criticism about Van Gogh again! All we have to do is look at the paintings.

And, of course, that vision, that possibility, that hope, is a blue anchor! It holds us fast, keeps us from being dashed upon the rocks, and is also the color of sky and of sadness.

The penultimate stanza is the most joyous: the survivors have somehow made it ashore, one, two, even three steps ashore. The waves, the tides will still be calling us back, but three steps: that's a foothold.

The final turn, surprising yet inevitable, in the last stanza, has always battered my heart (more than three times). That "wingprint" is a perfect word here, a perfect spondee, to describe the shadow of the mountain that someday might, that someday will, come falling down on our fragile settlement.

This poem has always struck me as a small masterpiece. I am glad to say that in print.

Note

1. Bill Knott.

LEE SHARKEY

"Threads: Rosa Luxemburg from Prison"

The urge among poets to pay homage to artists we love is common as cloth. We dedicate poems to them, quote them in poems, imitate their style or formal strategies; we enter their work and assume their voices. We engage them in conversation, generate ground where we can stand together, in history, outside of time.

Perhaps the deepest act of poetic homage is translation, or perhaps deep acts of poetic homage are themselves translations, acts of assimilation and devotion in which our own selves recede toward shadow. Jane Cooper's homages to Georgia O'Keeffe ("The Winter Road") and Willa Cather ("Vocation: A Life") are two such poems, employing the artists' words and work in multi-layered interplay. They reflect Cooper's immersion in that work and its creative sources, both geographical and biographical, her fascination with solitary women who made a mark on public life.

To my mind, the consummate example of homage in Cooper's poems is "Threads: Rosa Luxemburg from Prison," Cooper's rendering as English-language poetry of Luxemburg's prison letters to Sophie Liebknecht, the young wife of Karl Liebknecht, Luxemburg's imprisoned comrade. Luxemburg, the fiery revolutionary organizer, writer, and orator who cofounded the Spartacus League with Liebknecht and Rosa Zetkin, wrote prodigiously during the two and a half years she spent in prison for organizing workers' strikes against Germany's engagement in the First World War, which she saw as pitting the oppressed of opposing countries against each other. Her letters to her political comrades are often dense with political theory and calculus. But the letters to Liebknecht afford an intimate view of Luxemburg, who comes to life in "Threads" as an artist alert to the most minute phenomena in her circumscribed environment.

Yet, the Liebknecht letters already reveal this. Cooper has incorporated text from Eden and Cedar Paul's translation,[1] backgrounding herself completely. The imagery, ideas, and much of the phrasing are Luxemburg's, as if Cooper were an enthusiastic reader waving a favorite book in our face and insisting, *Look, look!* Cooper's choice to inhabit Luxemburg as literally as she does was a risky undertaking. The letters themselves contain vividly detailed descriptions and impassioned meditations; her effort might have resulted in a sort of copycat redundancy. It must have taken a high tolerance both for the risk of failure and for traveling blind through her own poetic process for Cooper to return to the project day after day and be consumed by it.

It has been instructive to me as both a poet and a reader of poetry to examine the strategies Cooper used to transform her material. Her main tool was the scalpel. She cut the chit chat ("How did you hear about your brother? through your mother, or direct?"), travel fantasies ("My plan is to carry you off to Corsica"), reminiscences of leisurely outings, readings Luxemburg recommends for Sophie's further education. She pared away the surplus intensifiers and descriptors common to speech and informal writing: "A large beetle was lying on its back and waving its legs helplessly, while a crowd of little ants were swarming round it and eating it alive!" results in "one day I found a beetle stunned on its back, / its legs gnawed to stumps by ants." Similes become metaphors. Sentences fragment. Meanderings concentrate. Onomatopoetic renderings of birdsong assume pride of place. One 375-word paragraph yields a single word, *zeezeebey*, the song of the blue tit, to insert into a different passage. What results is a stream of direct observation and personal reflection, the lyric "first self" (Luxemburg's term) within the self, the visionary within the revolutionary. An artist's soul emerges from the isolation of Luxemburg's imprisonment and reaches out to Sophie as to the beloved, in the voice of a mother, older sister, teacher, and emotional intimate.

The "threads" of the poem's title derive from Luxemburg's description in the letters of her empathic connection with all living beings. They also describe Cooper's compositional technique of dividing and recombining elements of the letters to heighten their immediacy. This passage from the May 2, 1917, letter from the Wronke prison is just one example:

I suppose I must be out of sorts to feel everything so deeply. Sometimes, however, it seems to me that I am not really a human being at all but like a bird or a beast in human form. I feel so much more at home even in a scrap of garden like the one here, and still more in the meadows when the grass is humming with bees than—at one of our party congresses. I can say that to you, for you will not promptly suspect me of treason to socialism! You know that I really hope to die at my post, in a street fight or in prison. But my innermost personality belongs more to my tom-tits than to the comrades.

Cooper reweaves the original to yield this stanza:

> Sonyusha, I know I can say this to you, my darling—
> You will not promptly accuse me
> of treason against socialism. Suppose I am really
> not a human being at all but some bird or beast?
> I walk up and down my scrap of prison garden—
> I'm alone in a field where the grass is humming with bees—
> and I feel more at home
> than at a party congress. Of course I always
> mean to die at my post, in a street fight
> or prison. But my first self
> belongs to the tomtits more than to our comrades

(159)

In one of her early poems,[2] Cooper poses the question, "Whom can we love in all these little wars?" dismissing the heroism of the sailor ("blind as a worm") and the aviator ("The sky is streaked with pilots falling"). We might read "Threads" as a response to that question, channeled through the figure of Luxemburg. The poem progresses through three sections, corresponding to sites and peri-ods of her imprisonment, moving as casually as thought from the birds and other animals she observes to her readings in natural sci-ence to philosophical musings to expressions of affection. In the first section, Luxemburg gently chides Sophie for her outrage at the authorities who kept her and Sophie's husband in "cages" for visits with family members. The blue tit's *zeezeebey* becomes her response to Sophie's corollary question, "*What is the meaning of it all?*"

> My little bird,
> given the totality of vital forms
> through twenty thousand years of civilization,
> that's not a reasonable question! Why are there blue tits?
> *Zeezeebey!* . . .

(159)

Threads of attention become visually distinct in the second section, where musings sparked by news of the death of Luxemburg's friend Hans Diefenbach at the front, bird migrations, and Luxemburg's assertions of "confident joy" at being part of something larger than herself form a left-justified thread:

> My cell trembles. I'm lying in a field streaked with light.
> How can that be? My heart beats. Life itself,
> the riddle, becomes the key to the riddle.
>
> (162)

These musings alternate with an indented thread of direct observation: a flock of rooks "homecoming" at twilight, then a narrative account of the torture of Romanian buffalos, "one ripped and bleeding / its stiff hide torn / the look on its black face like a weeping child's." The extent of Luxemburg's revolutionary project becomes clear: it must include the buffalo and the songbirds, must encompass the cataclysm of a war in which over 70 percent of the young men mobilized into the Russian, French, Romanian, and Austrian armies become its casualties ("this too must be transformed / into something meant, heroic"). Toward the end of the section, Cooper interjects the one passage in the poem she has invented whole cloth, an intense moment, we might imagine, of authorial empathy evoked by Luxemburg's empathy with the wounded buffalo. Prefiguring Luxemburg's assassination and the dumping of her corpse in Berlin's Landwehr Canal, Cooper writes—and here the syntax falters—

> Eyes
> of the bleeding My own dark
> handsomely photographed eyes
> Tears / negative
> Tears / negative
> Tears / negative of my own face dead
> skull beaten in and
> drowned
>
> (163–64)

This is the single moment in "Threads" in which the reader's attention is drawn to the difference, the distance, between the poet and her subject. There is no mention of a photographic portrait or negative of any kind in the Liebknecht letters. The interjected phrase "My own dark / handsomely photographed eyes" seems an awkward expression for someone to use about herself. I read this as Cooper's reminder to readers that the Luxemburg we may feel we are directly encountering on the page is a semblance: an act of authorial integrity at just the point where her channeling of her subject is most compelling.

In the concluding section, distilled from letters written during the spring of 1918 at Breslau Prison, compositional and thematic threads are closely interwoven. The war is coming to an end; "[f]ragments of the established world / flame and submerge, they tear away" (166) while Luxemburg remains in prison, unable to influence the ominous course of events. Nature is out of joint; the orioles have returned too soon, and their song has become uncanny. "*It's no use telling myself I am not responsible for all the hungry little larks in the world. Logic does not help*" (167), the Luxemburg persona writes, the sentence quoted verbatim from the actual Luxemburg's May 12 letter. The direct address to Sophie becomes more insistent in this section, conveying Luxemburg's need to bestow the protective shawl of her vision on her beloved young friend:

> This lovely world! If only we could walk through it, talk
> freely together weep over it. . . .
>   I fear you're driven,
> whipped by the winds of your loneliness,
> helpless as a young leaf. . . .
> Darling, the earth is faithful, the one thing
> fresh but yet faithful. Be my eyes for me,
> let me see all you see
> . . . .
>   I feel how   you must be suffering
> . . . .
>   suffering because you can't "live"
> . . . .
>   Never mind, we shall live   shall live
>   through grand events
>   Have patience
>
>   (165–67)

In a passage reminiscent of Adrienne Rich's "Planetarium," an homage to the astronomer Caroline Herschel ("I have been standing all my life in the / direct path of a battery of signals / the most accurately transmitted most / untranslatable language in the universe"), "Threads" approaches its conclusion:

> . . . passing out of my cell in all directions
> are fine threads connecting me
> with thousands of birds and beasts
>   You too, Sonitchka, are one of this urgent company . . .
>
>   (167)

Whom are we to love? Why "the totality of vital forms" that popu-
late the earth and cosmos? Then, deflating the rhetoric, in a gesture
typical of her work, Cooper ends the poem with what at first
sounds like an afterthought, the one recommendation for reading
she did not cull along with the many others that populate the let-
ters. Here, Cooper frames for Luxemburg a brief homage of her
own, an acknowledgment of debt to other writers:

> Perhaps Pfemfert can find you *The Flax Field*
> by Streuvels. For these Flemish authors
> not Flanders alone has become the beloved
> but all nature   beyond even
> the radiant skin
> of the globe
>
>   (167)

If in "Threads" "all nature" takes the form of the beloved, Rosa
Luxemburg is its ever-curious, mindful, even worshipful, witness
and ecstatic. Cooper has returned the concept of homage to its root
in the Latin word for earth, *humus,* passing on Luxemburg's pre-
scient ecological consciousness to a world ever more in need of it.
For homage also entails the impulse to transmit something irre-
placeable, not to let the radiance of those who came before us die
in the sloughs of history. In rendering this more complex portrait of
one of the twentieth century's most insightful political figures, the
poet has given us a Rosa Luxemburg who burns with tenderness
and inspires us to think and act.

Notes

   1. Available online at https://www.marxists.org/archive/luxemburg/
1918/letters-sophie.html
   2. "Meteors."

GALWAY KINNELL

Poets House Tribute to Jane Cooper

Jane Cooper belongs to that amazing line of American women po-
ets, which starts with Emily Dickinson and comes down to the
present—a line of poets who are daring, determined to know, and
not afraid of being personal; who are now transforming what
American poetry is; and who have made us realize that poetry is not
a past art but in important ways is in its infancy.

I came to know and admire and love Jane in the mid-1970s,
when I taught for several years at Sarah Lawrence. I know it's im-
modest of me to say so, but I *think* I became at a certain point a
fairly good teacher—and I date the change in my teaching from
those years at Sarah Lawrence when I occupied an office next to
Jane's and learned from Jane—from watching the careful, loving,
and—though I know she was often exhausted—the apparently in-
exhaustible attention she gave to the aspiring poets who arrived at
her door in steady successions—what may be the essence of all
teaching.

I wish I could speak at some length about Jane's poetry—but I
won't or I wouldn't have time to read any of her poems. But I need
to make these remarks about her poetry: the range of mood of her
poetry is very great; its voice is unusually intimate; and the poems
seem intent on articulating the full truth, however complex—
resulting sometimes in scalp-crawling moments when it seems the
poet has gone beyond what is possible to say, to walk out ahead of
knowing.

When I talked with Jane recently, she suggested I include a poem
by her friend Jane Kenyon, who lies very ill in a hospital in New
Hampshire. Visiting that Jane two weeks ago, I asked her about the
idea and she was thrilled. She helped choose the poem—and then,
apparently remembering some emotional inaccuracy she had dis-
covered in the poem after it had been published—looked alarmed.
"*But*—you're going to read this poem to Jane Cooper and there is
a lie in it! You must remember to change this line when you read it

. . . ." And she instructed me to make what seemed to me a very tiny substitution. For Jane K.—as for me and I'm sure many others—Jane C. represents a very high standard of truth-telling.

MARILYN CHIN

Notes on Precision
Remembering Jane Cooper

I am a perfectionist. Scratch that, I am a precisionist, obsessive when it comes to writing poetry. I revise and revise until my fingers bleed. I suspect that most good poets have this disorder. Certainly the ones I'm drawn to. This affliction first hit me bad in grad school in Iowa.

One day, walking from Don Justice's office to Jane Cooper's, I realized, "S%#!, both of my writing teachers write spare, unadorned lines, both generous of soul, but penurious of words." Neither of them published very much in their lifetimes because they were perfectionists. They knew too well what a "perfect" poem should look like and would not allow a flawed one to see light. Didn't let poems go too early, would rather burn them. I was quiet and shy, but a student who absorbed everything, especially my teachers' pain—the pain of judging one's own art so harshly.

That would be my best training. Every phoneme must be scrutinized. The Masters know when you are not being rigorous, when you are vapid of ideas and lazy with your lines, stuffing them with unwarranted modifiers. With Justice, it was all about craft. "This is cut up prose!" he would growl.

And Jane would quietly say, "Where are your poems? You haven't turned one in for a while." I once replied sardonically, "Oh, I'm stuck on a connective: *or* instead of *and*—." Jane was a very popular teacher with the women students; there was often a queue in front of her door. One time, I heard crying emanating from the other side of the door and recognized the tearful voice of one of my classmates. Jane was the soother of shattered egos. I would wait patiently at her door but, before attempting a knock, would imagine her contemplating a line. Did I dare disturb her quiet moments with the muse? I would retreat and go away.

Precise to a fault. When you are too self-conscious, you write yourself into a corner. You write the poem into paralysis. I once whittled a five-page poem into a haiku. And then threw out the haiku.

Obsessive, controlling, sexually frustrated, deathly afraid of failure—a "puritanical" signature, as Jane puts it. I'm sitting in my office at 3:00 a.m. rewriting a line twenty times while my comrades are at Sheep's Head drunk, flirting, having a great time—and still spitting out decent free verse poems in the morning to grace the "worksheet."

But as I grow older, I realize that precision is the secret of poetry. Both my affliction and my strength, my doom and salvation. I don't give a damn what others say about "process." For me, "process" is about finding precision. This journey might be interesting to watch, but it's a mess; and I can't deal with messes. My apartment can be all scattered, but my poems must be pristine.

I have been a student of Classical Chinese poetry all my life. I love the "jue-ju" line of only five characters. Classical Chinese grammar is concise, straightforward, bereft of connectives. No inflectional morphology, no excessive grammar.

Even as a baby on my grandmother's back, as she chanted Chinese poetry, I knew that each word in that ancient dialect was placed precisely. She memorized each exactly as it was sung to her. No jazzy riffs or improvisation with this grandmother! She was strict, uncompromising.

Here is one of my favorite five-character lines from Li Bai:

不 知 心 恨 誰
Don't know heart hates whom

Perfect. It kills! Slays! Perfectly describing a woman's anguish! I carried these characters in my pocket for several months, chanting them in three different dialects.

Precision is always hermetic, full of anxiety, never liberating. I would go for months without writing a single poem, hold on to drafts too long, refusing to let go. I have fifty poems in the drawer yearning to be finished. They gnaw at my conscience constantly. I shout back to them, "You are finished when I say you are finished." On my cranky days, I try to blame Justice and Cooper and Tang dynasty poets and even my tyrannical grandmother!

Would I have been less anxious about writing had I learned from Whitman? And Ginsberg, who declared that he did not revise! Would I have been a different writer had I had Olson as mentor? As for the Chinese, perhaps I should have loved the Fu over the jue-ju, the long-winded digressive parallel couplets instead of cut-verse quatrains.

But precision: a short quatrain from Emily Dickinson says everything about God.

A few years after I graduated, I visited Jane Cooper in her spare New York apartment. I brought miniature yellow roses; she offered tea and biscuits. I felt so warmly appreciated in that apartment. Once again, she asked, "Where are your poems? Did you bring me a new poem?" And so, I did, in my red book bag. I didn't want to disappoint her. I had spent all week polishing a short lyric and as I read it out loud, I realized that I could have cut the first two stanzas. Eureka! But Jane just nodded and said nothing.

A week ago, I reread one of my favorite Jane Cooper poems.

RENT

If you want my apartment, sleep in it
but let's have a clear understanding:
the books are still free agents.

If the rocking chair's arms surround you
they can also let you go,
they can shape the air like a body.

I don't want your rent, I want
a radiance of attention
like the candle's flame when we eat,

I mean a kind of awe
attending the spaces between us—
Not a roof but a field of stars.

(154)

A deceptively simple poem, but how precise! She generously offers her small New York apartment with spare furniture but on her terms. How the small apartment opens up to "a field of stars" is pure magic. I love and cherish it! Can't quibble with it, not even with the colon.

"If the rocking chair's arms surround you / they can also let you go" is a nuanced ambiguity. Coded, for her students. We were sojourners, passing tourists, and shouldn't stay too long. I was projecting my own anxieties all along. In my sixth decade, can I finally let go?

JENNY FACTOR

Inhabiting

*Lessons from Jane Cooper's Spacious
Architectures*

If you want my apartment, sleep in it
but let's have a clear understanding:
the books are still free agents.

(154)

So begins "Rent," one of Jane Cooper's many poems that ruminate
about *structures* both architectural and human. This invitation to
sublet (and likely cohabit) an apartment becomes carnal with ani-
mated objects (the books have souls, the rocking chair has arms);
the poem itself seems a negotiation of walls, words, and bone. But
most important, in this little chamber, the shapes (books, chair)
make possible a fluid, refining focus on their *opposites*: not the *co-
inhabiting other* but, rather, potential fluid air:

If the rocking chair's arms surround you
they can also let you go,
they can shape the air like a body.

"Rent" appears in Cooper's third published book, *Scaffolding,*
whose very title is architectural. But poems as early as "The Builder
of Houses" (in which a child seeks out and is forced to abandon a
series of small personal "homes") and "In the Last Moments Came
the Old German Cleaning Woman" place identity and relationships
in a meditation on place and architecture. And later poems, like
"Dispossessions" ("Last night a voice called me from outside my
door. / It was no one's voice, perhaps it came from the umbrella
stand" and "Houses, houses, we lodge in such husks!" 132–33) con-
tinue animating objects, juxtaposing people and space. Each organic
unit has room for prevarication, multivalence, world-seeing, even
humor; each poem defines a region of space and air.

For Cooper, poetry—from individual poems to creative practice—holds not something fixed but spacious potentiality, not bars (marriage, commitment, expectations, rituals, rent checks) but radical openness ("a radiance of attention" . . . "a kind of awe / attending the spaces between us").

With poems so shapely, and even at times formal, it's unexpected for the lesson to be spaciousness and wander. But in the final tabulation, that's what I (a young poet writing in verse form) learned from Jane Cooper's (formal and open) work. To see this potential in Jane Cooper's *poetry* is one thing; to learn from it from her person is another.

As a poet living briefly in New York City in the 1990s, I was in my own time of space and air. For writers coming of age in the 1990s, especially those asking New York City to serve as their canvas and school, the role and resonance of Jane Cooper was present in the City—from her poems (crafty, honorable, smart) to her persona (that cool grace, and the sense she seemed to make of a life committed to art). We younger poets were in that decade (or more) of work that I think builds a poet—a kind of phenomenon of creative focus. But unlike us, that phenomenon had happened for Cooper *twice* in her youth (first in her early twenties in Florida after the war when she wrote a book she didn't publish, and then again when she attended the University of Iowa purportedly to learn to teach fiction but ultimately to transform herself). Her respect for that period-of-work—in herself and others—its fluidity, intensity, and importance—seemed well-established and well-known, and served as a point of potential meeting. She could be approached, we knew; and when she was, she was known to treat younger poets in a way that was both helpful and still judging, pointing, permitting, but directional.

I did not attend Sarah Lawrence College. So while I knew Jane Cooper's work and presence around the City by reputation, I did not at first interact with her as a teacher or a friend.

However, on an evening in January in a year after 2000, I *did* at last meet Jane Cooper and receive some wisdom from her. The day had been a stormy one. I sloshed through a slushy, still-falling snow so deep it had shut down all three New York City airports to read poems with Jane Cooper and Marilyn Hacker at a tiny East Village reading space. The reading series, MAKOR, was sponsored and curated by the talented Eve Grubin, a poet herself, who was bringing together a type of "mentor string" for this series—creating a dialogue of mostly Jewish poets in which she felt one poet (in this case, Cooper, whose work was interested in Jewish themes) had given something important to another (Marilyn Hacker) who had given something important (mentorship, friendship) to the third poet reading that night (me).

As the junior poet, I read first, sharing new poems that were not yet published in a book. The second-to-the-final one was a longish poem in Sapphics.[1] That long poem—I'd never read it in public before, and it seemed to choke me. That happens sometimes. A poem that had been just fine on a page or in a practice starts to feel frightening or boring or unspeakable at a reading.

I was discovering that night the sensation for the first time: the room hushed (bored? I wondered). The poem took its time. It had shame in it. A shame built of its lung-i-ness; the need to abide with myself in saying it, in writing it, in putting it out there. The poem told the story of a hike I didn't take with a group of women on a moonstruck night ("I'm no longer anyone's perfect daughter / I'm no Jewish matriarch of a long chain. / See me climb down mountains to keep my face in / Family albums"); it came from my real self, given room.

Jane Cooper's work had a maturity that just soared that evening—it was quiet, significant; we knew we were hearing an important poet's voice. Marilyn Hacker was dulcet-voiced, her poems political, brave, and linguistically inventive. My reading was fine, not better, and I was fully aware of it.

After the reading, and before heading home, Jane called me over to say a few words. I don't remember the words precisely, but as I recall it, she told me the work I'd read was fine, but that really only one of the poems was better than that. She wanted me to know which one, because perhaps I'd want to write more. To my surprise, the poem she singled out was the long, hard one: the Sapphics.

I knew from what she said and how she said it that she didn't have a particularly personal emotional reaction to my poems, except maybe the only one I didn't want anyone to love. I could have felt disappointed, or embarrassed or hurt. But I didn't. There was something so teacherly and earnest in the feedback that I trusted it as one would trust any completely true and honorable thing.

Jean Valentine, in a 1997 introduction to the work of Jane Cooper, wrote: "There is another line of Willa Cather's that Jane Cooper quotes, that describes her own work for me: 'Artistic growth is, more than it is anything else, a refining of the sense of truth-fulness.'"[2]

And so in the helpful way caring critique can, the comment sat with me for a long time.

A few years later, in 2003, I reviewed *Flashboat: Poems Collected and Reclaimed* for *Prairie Schooner*. I discovered it to be a book about process—which is, if you think about it, pretty radical stuff. Most *Collected Poems* aim toward commodification: the poet's life and work in airbrushed retrospective. The goal is to position an author and their work in the sense of *oeuvre* and canon.

Cooper had something else in mind. She includes poems she rejected earlier, revises poems, and amply explains acts of creation in essay and note. Cooper is aiming for process not product in the title of the essay "Nothing Has Been Used in the Manufacture of This Poetry . . ." Though taken from a war scarcity slogan, the title also functions as a refusal of commodification. It seems to say, "Nothing in this book is made from the stuff of products" (consumables)—an anti-consumerism that speaks to us today.

What I admire in *The Flashboat* are Cooper's many gestures of questioning, which I experience as a radical spaciousness, including her willingness to explore childhood in all its losses. I love how even in the personal bereavement poem "In the House of the Dying," loss is strange and partially processed; in fact, never are these poems processed past honesty, beyond what anyone can genuinely know of themselves or one another.

We know we are in a *process* book, too, when we read the volume's subtitle (poems "collected and *reclaimed*") and *then* at the dedication page, where Cooper writes:

For Grace, Adrienne, Jean
>   *My friends are my "estate."*
>   – E.D. TO SAMUEL BOWLES
>   *(1858?)*

The list of names are so distinctive, we *think* we know to whom she is referring. But the mention of each woman's name is personal, private, and partial. We can guess who these friends are—Grace (Paley), Adrienne (Rich), Jean (Valentine)—but Cooper is not trying to tell us, really, who they are, but rather to call out to *them* directly. And the quote is attributed to "E.D."—rather than Emily Dickinson. We know who "E.D." is, either by abbreviated convention or by being familiar with the *only* complete name on the page—Samuel Bowles—possibly the least well-known of the five, and the only male, and yet the only one not in ellipse. In fact, the elliptical here is clearly richer (and more seditious) than the part that's spelled out. The year Dickinson said this is left not as fact but as a kind of dialogue. Who but a person with very pronounced and personal aesthetics would publish a date with the year still listed as a question mark?

It seems to me that almost any significant career in writing happens after the poet enters a flashpoint of obsessive focus and study—a significant sequence of years in which the emerging writer emits a special sort of energy, a preoccupation with the internal dialogue of words. This time is as physically and intimately receptive as the amorous time of late adolescence—when affections can be flamed in solipsistic silence and nurtured without fertile reciprocation over months or decades. The organism of the artist is sensitive then in the way young lovers are. The artist is listening hard. From this burning youthful entanglement, an artist is born.

Part of what makes Jane Cooper so special is that she seems (to me) to have remained in that state, not only during her two times of "becoming" but throughout a long career. The stunning poem "The Flashboat" describes this ("work, the starry waters") as a choice—as craft *given room* to become the decision, the night place, the effort. When she spoke to me that night, I was in my own period of radical aesthetic openness. And so like an amorous adolescent, I *did* hear both the words and the stony thing underneath them.

And what I came to understand was that I had to bring air into my architectures, even at great personal risk. I had to let boring happen in the poem-process. I had to let "not enough" happen in the poem process. I had to be *me*—human, not laser-like; textured, not shiny. Over the course of a long, patient career, or a single spacious but shapely poem, I had to refuse arrival and commodification and give my musing *room*.

I came to understand something about poetry as a *process*. And about poetry as a *life choice*. And perhaps the bravest thing after all was—not shining—but rather staying. This Cooper-ian aesthetics of work and process, clean walls and honest contained self is a remarkable compass indeed.

In her early poem "A Little Vesper," Cooper writes, "It's time to . . . / bed with what we are." I think that's it, exactly. I think my life since then has been a long, resistant arc into accepting that as a style, a truth, and a poem-process.

The poem "Rent" concludes in a sphere of openness:

I don't want your rent, I want
a radiance of attention
. . .
Not a roof but a field of stars.

(154)

If my Sapphics hiked out into a place of wandering and connection,
structure (the Sapphic form) and air (the meandering fantasy) are
perhaps why Jane Cooper responded to them. Stargazing points
indistinctly upward. We take a breath. The poem is a room *full* of
time and breath. Scaffolded by language, we head out to connect to
that dark unstructured space.

Notes

1. Jenny Factor, "A Cold, High, Bright Full Moon," *Unraveling at the
Name,* (Port Townsend: Copper Canyon Press, 2002).
2. Jean Valentine Papers, 1952–2004; Jane Cooper, 1997. MC 538, folder
6.2. Schlesinger Library, Radcliffe Institute, Harvard University, Cam-
bridge, Mass.

LISA SACK

Angle of Repose
Jane Cooper's Long View

Czeslaw Milosz once said that when the religious imagination
erodes, writers turn to poetry, because in poems they can address
questions—about mortality and eternity—that have no answers.
For Jane Cooper, an American poet who recently turned seventy,
such questions are central to her new collection, *Green Notebook,
Winter Road*. Friends have died or are dying (she dedicates the book
to, among others, Muriel Rukeyser and Shirley Eliason Haupt), and
Cooper, herself suffering from an immune deficiency, hasn't en-
joyed the best of health. Death infuses these poems and prose pieces
with a compelling urgency and honesty, as if, in its presence, Coo-
per dropped what little pretense she had and scoured her life and
the English language for truth.

"The Green Notebook," which opens the volume—and, like all
good beginnings, is a seductive invitation to the reader—announces
the meticulous and uncompromising journey about to start:

> There are 64 panes in each window of the Harrisville church
> where we sit listening to a late Haydn quartet. . . .
> . . . the evening sky
> glistens like the pink inside of a shell over uncropped grass,
> over a few slant graves.

Cooper inhabits a world where death hovers behind the natural
splendors of life: "At Sargent Pond the hollows are the color of
strong tea. / Looking down you can see decomposed weeds and the
muscular bronze and green / stems of some water lilies." In this odd
balance, the poet finds herself

> . . . on the edge
> of discovering the green notebook containing all the poems of my
>   life,
> I mean the ones I never wrote. The meadow turns intensely green.

The notebook is under my fingers. I read. My companions read.
Now thunder joins in, scurry of leaves. . . .

How can the reader, arriving, after a series of exquisite images, at
that blunt statement of failure ("I mean the ones I never wrote"),
not feel a pang of grief for herself as well as the writer? Yet Coo-
per hasn't given up: even as this autumnal book takes stock of her
life—as artist, friend, and Southerner—and sometimes finds it
wanting, she trembles with anticipation. In poetry, in the careful
observation and recording of the world, Cooper can transform
herself.

Even with this understanding, hers has been a slow and painstak-
ing passage. In the last twenty-five years, Cooper, who taught for
many years at Sarah Lawrence and helped to invent its writing pro-
gram, has published only three books: *Scaffolding: New and Selected
Poems* (Anvil Press Poetry Ltd., London, 1984), *Maps & Windows*
(Macmillan, 1974), and *The Weather of Six Mornings* (1969), which was
the Lamont Poetry Selection for 1968. The two later books include
previously published poems and only a handful of newer poems. So
it's no wonder fans have impatiently awaited *Green Notebook, Winter
Road*. Fortunately, strangers to Cooper's work won't have to hunt far
for her older poems. Tilbury House printed the first American edi-
tion of *Scaffolding* in 1993, giving readers new and old the opportu-
nity to see the birth of a distinctive American voice.

As the title suggests, *Scaffolding* examines the process of making
poetry even as it presents the finished work. The book is Cooper's
life story: great expanses of silence surround the chronologically
arranged poems. She fully acknowledges the difficulties she's had as
a writer. Even though the number of poems is small, their force and
intelligence have kept Cooper's career aloft all this time. Her desire
for and willingness to change leap off every page of both *Scaffolding*
and *Green Notebook, Winter Road*, but no transformation is greater
than Cooper's decision to shake off the mantle of the British tradi-
tion. Her early poems are highly formal, modeled on Yeats, Hop-
kins, Auden, and Spender. Sometime in the mid-1960s she realized
that their "half-borrowed rhetorical style" didn't suit her, that "no
choice is absolute and no structure can save us." Conducting a one-
woman Boston Tea Party, Cooper threw out rhetoric and rhyme in
favor of free verse. For the reader wading through *Scaffolding*, the
sudden encounter with open lines is like the slap of ice-cold moun-
tain water against warm skin—heart-stopping and invigorating.

That's not to say that Cooper's formal poems are dull, but compared to the free verse, they feel mannered and very well-behaved. Think of Isadora Duncan bound up in a corset and too-tight shoes.

Here's the opening of "Morning on the St. John's," Cooper's blank-verse sestina: "This is a country where there are no mountains: / At dawn the water birds like lines of rain / Rise from the penciled grasses by the river / And slantwise creak across the growing light. / The sky lifts upward and the breath of flowers / Wakes with the shadows of the waking birds." Compare the elegant, stately roll of those lines to the curt, searing movement of "Letters":

> That quiet point of light
> trembled and went out.
>
> Iron touches a log:
> it crumbles to coal, then ashes.
>
> The log sleeps in its shape.
> A new moon rises.
>
> Darling, my white body
> still bears your imprint.

Its very abstemiousness gives "Letters" mystery and force; the verbs glint. By stripping away artifice, Cooper—like her more famous colleagues and admirers, Adrienne Rich and Galway Kinnell—found a truer voice.

Though stylistic liberation came late, liberation as a theme did not. It is one of Cooper's primary and most flammable topics. She has never married or had children; in her poems and essays, Cooper tussles with the consequences of her choices. Many of the poems have a distinctly androgynous quality, suggesting the quest of liberation goes way beyond sexuality. And even precedes sexuality: first, one has to voice her right to be free. The early poems investigate boundaries between the self and others: "Here I am yours, and here, and here: . . . And here I am not yours"; "You pray / For marriage as another man might pray / For sleep after surgery . . . you won't believe / There is any other way to live / Than whole . . ."; "I expose / And kill and heal you with the simplest finger. / I'm radium, apocalypse in the breast."

Cooper then had to declare her right to write. The 1974 essay "Nothing Has Been Used in the Manufacture of This Poetry That

Could Have Been Used in the Manufacture of Bread," in which she asks why so many women writers suppress or belittle their work, and how they are to balance their needs as artists and women, is no less valid or acute today than it was twenty years ago. In Cooper's case, the scales tilted towards the artist's needs: "My body knows it will never bear children. / What can I say to my body now / . . . Let compassion breathe in and out of you / filling you and / singing."

These subjects—artistic and personal freedom—have receded as death has become primary. In *Green Notebook, Winter Road*, Cooper seeks to escape mortality. She wills herself to face it, along with illness, and the past. Poetry is her sacred path. "I'm trying," she says, "to write a poem that will alert me to my very real life."

> It would have to be a poem dense with ordinary detail
> the way the sun, spilling across walnut and balled-up napkins,
> can pick out cups, plates . . .
> . . . with evenhanded curiosity. . . .

Stubborn and exacting, Cooper always begins with what's seen and waits patiently until the unexpected and unseen reveals itself. There's evanescence to the writing: sometimes the truths she discovers are so delicate and elusive, you want to trap them before they evaporate. What anchors Part I, "On the Edge of the Moment," is the interconnection between the poems: poems written to and about dead or dying friends and family. Cooper carries a phrase or an idea from one page to the next, so that this section—the strongest in the book—moves forward as if by association. Just as she strings individual words together to "arrive at . . . truth," Cooper strings poems, too: "On the Edge of the Moment" is an extended mediation on loss.

In Part II, "Family Stories," Cooper delves into her past. Addressing her dead friend Muriel Rukeyser and James Wright, she asks with uncharacteristic heavy-handedness, "tell me how to redress the past, / how to relish yet redress / my sensuous, precious, upper-class, / unjust white child's past." Such a frontal assault seems, at least to this reader, at odds with, and less effective than, the diligent accumulation of observed details employed elsewhere. Cooper's "complex shame" at being Southern ("It's like being German") shows itself plainly enough in the way she relates the tales.

"Give Us This Day" (Part III) pairs a poem describing Cooper's present-day illness with a memoir about her childhood sickness,

"The Children's Ward." Originally published in *Extended Outlooks: The Iowa Review Collection of Contemporary Women Writers*, which Cooper coedited, "The Children's Ward" succeeds at the hardest of balancing acts—conveying a child's sensibility without sacrificing the depth and insight of an adult perspective.

Cooper closes *Green Notebook, Winter Road* with two long poems about Georgia O'Keeffe and Willa Cather. Both are fascinating, not just for their insights into the work of the painter and the novelist but for the light they shed on Cooper herself. Readers unfamiliar with Cather's novels may find "Vocation: A Life" obscure, but no one can mistake Cooper's intent, speaking as O'Keeffe, in "The Winter Road": "Where I have been is of no importance ... // ... Where I was born is of no importance ... // Only what I have made of it / what I have been able to finish ...." While Jane Cooper hasn't produced a voluminous body of work, what she has finished is substantial. She's outwitted death—that most impossible of tasks—by preserving, for eternity, both seen and unseen moments.

EVE GRUBIN

Jane Cooper and the Poetics of Sanity

A tall painting of a cluttered artist's studio hung on the main wall of
Jane Cooper's tidy living room. The painting depicted a room filled
with canvases and objects and a rug spread out over the floor, a large
shadowed crease folded at the rug's center. During a visit, we dis-
cussed the painting, and Jane smiled and said, "Adrienne Rich has
astutely observed that the crease is the only wrinkle in my home."

That wrinkle in Jane Cooper's neat home represents how she
entered a poem. Her characteristic orderliness allowed her, para-
doxically, to notice sweet disorder, to pay attention to chaos amidst
the fearful symmetry; this noticing led to poems of wild civility.
Cooper was interested in observation, in seeing the real—in all of
its mess, simplicity, and splendor—in embracing, with clarity, what
lies before us, in what she called, "the sanity of observed detail"
(118).

Jane Cooper's poems honor, sometimes with gravity and some-
times with delight, the bounty of what the world has to offer. Don-
ald Revell writes, "What need for invention? . . . The eye does not
invent the light; there's no need. The mind makes no materials; it
doesn't have to . . . poems rejoice—in particular, in detail."[1]

Cooper had no "need for invention" as the surrealists did. The
sensibility in her poems reflects affection for the sanity of reality. In
her essay "Nothing Has Been Used in the Manufacture of This
Poetry That Could Have Been Used in the Manufacture of Bread,"
she writes that she spent the winter and spring of 1952–53 simply
taking notes in her journal as she looked out of her New York City
windows (119). Like a painter, looking was what she aimed for:
"truly looking at the world around me," she writes, "and trying to
record it." She writes in the essay that she is particularly moved by
John Crowe Ransom's "notion that it is the specific detail, inti-
mately rendered that reveals our love for the subject." Her poems
were not interested in fabrication or fantasy. Meditating on the gift
of the real led to poems of luminous attention. Here is the first
stanza of "Ordinary Detail" (174):

I'm trying to write a poem that will alert me to my real life,
a poem written in the natural speech of the breakfast table,
of a girl spooning yogurt, pausing, the spoon held aloft
while she gestures toward the exact next turning of her thought.

For Cooper, connecting to the truth of "real life" involved an unaffected expression in "natural speech" attending to the quotidian: e.g., "the breakfast table," "yogurt," "the spoon." In the next stanza, she writes,

It would have to be a poem dense with ordinary detail
the way the sun, spilling across walnut and balled-up napkins,
can pick out cups, plates, the letter from which someone has just
    read aloud,
with evenhanded curiosity, leaving behind a gloss of pleasure.

The sun spills across the homeliest of items, highlighting their creases—the "balled-up napkins" are like the wrinkled rug in the painting in her living room. Cooper's poems wake us up to the reality of our lives. This quality can be found in the art by some of the painters who worked in New York during her time—Jane Freilicher and Fairfield Porter, for instance. John Ashbery's recent piece on Freilicher's "Untitled: Still Life with a Copy of ARTnews," could apply to a Cooper poem. He wrote about the "still life that brings together a half-dozen miscellaneous objects, including a few roses that are having the floral equivalent of a bad hair day. . . ."[2] When describing what lay before her, Cooper was interested in all details, including the things that were having the "equivalent of a bad hair day." She wrote in her essay that "what poetry must do is alert us to a truth, and it must be necessary; once it exists, we realize how much we needed exactly this" (111).

Jane Cooper's poems not only honor the reality of the seen world as they de-sentimentalize everyday items, but they also scrutinize the hidden. The mysteries that lie in the dark are just as real in her poems as the items the sun illuminates on the breakfast table. The third stanza of "Ordinary Detail" begins with the line, "And yet this poem too must allow for the unseen" (174). Earlier in the poem, in the last lines of the first two stanzas, the unseen is hinted at.

The last line of the first stanza, "she gestures toward the exact next turning of her thought," placed after the list of items on the breakfast table, suggests that the unseen inner life, in this case, thought—the intellectual life—is as substantial, valuable, and unimagined as the physical world. The elegant dance of a woman's unseen mind is captured in the language: her "gestures" and her "turning" thoughts. The poem is emphatic that the "next thought" (implying a link with previous thoughts) is "exact." There is nothing vague, nothing that is not a part of "real life" when it comes to the inner life. It is precise, true, and impeccable: "exact."

In the last lines of the second stanza, "the letter from which someone has just read aloud, / with evenhanded curiosity, leaving behind a gloss of pleasure," the poem merges the sanity of the seen and the unseen. The sun illuminates a physical letter, but the reader has arrived too late to hear the words read from it. The scene is both clear and mysterious. The outcome is a wild sanity, an "evenhanded curiosity." There is a sane beauty, a "pleasure," in balance, evenness, and calm when married to curiosity and the wrinkled elegant turning of thoughts.

It is no coincidence that the figure in this painterly poem is a woman. Jane's deep concern with the lives of women can be found in her essays, poems, and conversations she had with friends and interviewers. She came of age as a writer during a time when American men had just returned from the war and women were expected to return to the kitchens. At the same time, the seeds of the women's movement and the sexual revolution were growing. These cultural and social pressures, she argued, led to complicated and painful choices for women and much suffering. She famously wrote, "The women poets I read about were generally not known for their rich, stable sexual and family lives" (114). Jane's acute awareness of this painful reality, a life's work that explored its complexities, and her own life of dignity and integrity allowed her to represent, for the next generation of women poets, a model of an elegantly sane and empathetic woman poet.

Jane's wild civility, evenhanded curiosity, and that carefully observed wrinkle in a studio of cluttered artwork in her tidy apartment created the perfect balance of wildness and sanity for negative capability to blossom. She wrote, "A poem uses everything we know, the surprising things we notice, whatever we can't solve that keeps on growing . . ." (112).

Notes

1. Donald Revell, *The Art of Attention: A Poet's Eye* (St Paul, Minn.: Graywolf, 2009), 14.
2. John Ashbery, "Jane Freilicher: (1924–2014)," *Artforum*. Jan 19, 2015.

GAIL MAZUR

"The Green Notebook"

There are 64 panes in each window of the Harrisville church
where we sit listening to a late Haydn quartet. Near the ceiling
    clouds
build up, slowly brightening, then disperse, till the evening sky
glistens like the pink inside of a shell over uncropped grass,
over a few slant graves.

(173)

Three blizzards into the unrelenting winter of 2015, it's exhilarating
to immerse myself in the three stanzas, of irregular lines, of Jane
Cooper's mid-summer poem. Cooper, in her sixties when she
wrote it, and well aware of the passage of time, listens to the late
music of Haydn in a New England church. Light pours in from
sixty-four-paned windows (was she sixty-four?) suffusing the cha-
pel. "The Green Notebook" is at once celebratory (nature and art)
and valedictory (*late, evening, hollows, scurry of leaves*, etc.).

It is early evening, sunset. Indoors and outdoors are fused by the
light, ceiling and sky are one and the same. Exterior, interior, painted
by the same hand.

The mind's eye of the poet moves from its acknowledgment of
evening, its pearlescent light, to the few, askew graves and the un-
tended grass—in the church graveyard? With a ceiling of "bright-
ening" clouds, nature itself becomes chapel, chapel becomes nature,
and late Haydn—probing, inventive, a little dark—becomes a kind
of hymn to it. A magical quietude prevails, a quietude pulsing with
life. The poet's eye takes it in, the ear and heart.

At Sargent Pond the hollows are the color of strong tea.
Looking down you can see decomposed weeds and the muscular
    bronze and green
stems of some water lilies. Out there on the float
three figures hang between water and air, the heat breathes them,
    they no longer speak.
It is a seamless July afternoon.

127

The second stanza moves out into the *late* July landscape, the eye's imagination gets tougher, the pond's an arena of density and attrition, its growth decomposing, its watery depths a deep brown. The water lilies at their peak, bronze and muscular. Ethereality is not part of the natural world envisaged here. Cooper's point of view shifts, yet seamlessly, from the traditional peace of the church interior, to the life she can only, in this moment, look at, look for, or imagine.

Youthful (we guess) figures on a float yet also floating, the heat of summer an atmosphere so natural to the three that it breathes them. Sensuality, dense, heated, suspended, and also timeless—yet floating toward fate. Midsummer of youth.

Is there wistfulness in the voice of this poem? I don't think so, not even here, although a wise friend has said to me that it's really about death. But I find, rather, an appetite for, an awareness and appreciation of, the bodily and aesthetic pleasures of the season. And more, almost a song of praise for the world Cooper's taking in and being taken in by (I keep being reminded of Lorca's "Green, I Love You Green." Or Marvell's "*Annihilating all that's made / To a green thought in a green shade . . .*").

Greenness is all. But is it? No. Light and darkness. Joy and grief. Life and attrition. And that unfashionable value, beauty, a beauty about to be ravished, I find ravishing.

> Nameless. Slowly gathering. . . . It seems I am on the edge
> of discovering the green notebook containing all the poems of my
>   life,
> I mean the ones I never wrote. The meadow turns intensely green.
> The notebook is under my fingers. I read. My companions read.
> Now thunder joins in, scurry of leaves. . . .

This final stanza acknowledges the anonymity and therefore, maybe, the universality of the floating figures, of the provenance of what the poet sees and imagines. And "nameless" moves her to the sense of her work, of naming, work she has spent her life shaping, deepening, perfecting; and to the sense of work yet to be written. The line break (*my life, / I mean*) first implies the notebook contains her life's work—then undoes the achievement: everything in it is unwritten.

All this time of the poem, Cooper has been reading the world, she's been experiencing the greenness of it *as* the notebook containing poems she never wrote. Rueful, a melancholy idea. Annihilating.

Has she not captured its greenness?

No, but she is on the verge of it, of transcribing what her fingers, her senses have discovered. As if it were braille and she could read it: *the notebook under my fingers.* And she does read, companioned and yet solitary. The life of the artist, the life of making, is ongoing. Beginnings are a gift! She's in it, and in the poem. Time is hurrying: *Now thunder joins in, scurry of leaves. . . .* No matter.

(A few poems later in *The Flashboat,* there's a poem called "Long, Disconsolate Lines," in memory of Jane Cooper's friend Shirley Eliason. "The Green Notebook" seems to me a poem of long, uncommonly consoling lines.)

The Family Stories of Jane Cooper

From the beginning of her writing life, Jane Cooper used family recollections and misdemeanors as a stimulus for her poems. "For My Mother in Her First Illness, from a Window Overlooking Notre Dame" and "My Young Mother" both appeared in her first collection, *The Weather of Six Mornings*. These poems, and others, set Cooper on a course, not only of reflection but of realization and acceptance of the circumstances in her life as well as the lives of her relatives and the times in which they lived.

Cooper presages the ruminations that will be fully developed in *Green Notebook, Winter Road* in its opening poem, saying "It seems I am on the edge / of discovering the green notebook containing all the poems of my life, / I mean the ones I never wrote" ("The Green Notebook," 173). Cooper's intention to correct that omission as well as to overcome an earlier fear is fulfilled in the "Family Stories" section of *Green Notebook* ("I suspect most privately of all, I couldn't face living out the full range of intuition [my poems] revealed," she had written earlier, in the essay "Nothing Has Been Used in the Manufacture of This Poetry That Could Have Been Used in the Manufacture of Bread").

The poems included in the second section of *Green Notebook* don't merely revolve around blood relations but also, with the first poem, recognize a broad definition of family. In "Hotel de Dream" (189–90), Cooper identifies James Wright and Muriel Rukeyser (the latter to whom, among others, *Green Notebook* is dedicated) as "justice-keepers," wishing she could "telephone the dead." Cooper names these "friends of my choosing years" as those with whom she'd like to walk and talk, whose guidance she seeks in order to learn how to redress her "upper-class / unjust white child's past." It is noteworthy that Cooper chooses to undertake this self-evaluation through the lenses of Wright (who recalled in "Autumn Begins in Martins Ferry, Ohio" the "gray faces of Negroes in the blast furnace at Benwood") and Rukeyser (whose literary roots were planted, in part, when she was a journalist covering the 1932 trial of the black

Scottsboro youths accused of raping two white girls and on which she based her poem "The Trial"). The unavoidable conclusion is that issues of race and secret conflicts within the familial context haunted Cooper throughout her lifetime (she was seventy years old when *Green Notebook* was published) and harken back to Rukeyser's belief that in secret conflicts lie inescapable poems.

Cooper is straightforward about her task, as reflected in the section's third poem, "From the Journal Concerning My Father." This multi-part prose poem hinges on early impressions, Cooper's understanding of the world deriving from the maps that hung in her Florida childhood home, and the stories that created them. No devotee to rigid form, Cooper remembers family beyond the confines of her upbringing, realizing that a family's shape is fluid. Identifying, in "The Hobby Lobby" (198–99), a relative who made an appearance at the 1939 World's Fair and using tercets appropriate to the mother-father-child troika which is critical to the poem, Cooper reveals the parents' sense of superiority concerning distant relatives ("my father's second cousin / once removed") who put their homegrown artistry on public display for all the world to see. And in a five-line poem pointedly entitled "Class" (200), Cooper contrasts a grandmother's "old black Packard" with a "fisherman's daughter" who "owned no drawers." As with the previous poem, Cooper makes no judgment; she just provides observation, though her choice to record these particular observations about class distinctions amounts to a kind of judgment.

Just after Cooper has lulled the reader with the comfortable ease of the prose and free verse in the first six poems of "Family Stories," she turns to the formal by appropriating African American blues—presumably and effectively reflecting the poem's subject matter—in "Wanda's Blues" (201). The poem is the payoff for "Class," as it describes the life lived by the daughter of a railway man—a wandering life in which Wanda swept and cooked and sewed for a father who was often away from home. The speaker's repetition of the daughter's name—"*Wanda Wanda*"—coupled with the description of it as an "American refrain" (author's emphasis) speaks to Cooper's understanding of the repetitive lack of comfort in Wanda's life and its thread-line throughout the tapestry of 1930s America.

As though to better illuminate the worlds described in "The Hobby Lobby" and "Wanda's Blues," Cooper again turns her gaze toward her family and childhood home—and herself—their complicity and actions in the face of the milieu of her youth. In "The

Past" (202), Cooper resurrects a time when she could "reach back and rummage in the 19th century," reflecting on Cousin Josiah, a Congressman who spoke of "two ancient people of color" who had been born on the "family place," and Josiah's son, a Quaker who won safe conduct from the Gestapo. Cooper's poems recognize that these pieces of knowledge give rise to more questions than answers. She muses "how do I connect in my own body . . . which already spans a couple of centuries?" and wonders: "how soon will my body . . . become almost transparent and begin to shiver apart?" presumably understanding the potential loss of history if she doesn't record it.

Notwithstanding or perhaps because of the realization of her own mortality, Cooper concedes that her perception of the world is rooted in "Being Southern" (203), which, she dryly notes, is "like being German": you must acknowledge the guilt even when it is not your own. Cooper's willingness to take this stand—even in the 1990s—was a courageous one that, even today, is not often acknowledged by Southerners raised in the kind of environment and privilege in which she was raised. Cooper is willing to face her guilt head-on, declaring that those around her—family and neighbors—were "paternalistic," and that she "honor[ed] their accomplishments" and, once transplanted to the North, "never questioned [the] town." Most notably in these poems, Cooper doesn't make excuses; and, as evidenced by the tone of these poems, is only a little surprised and, more often, saddened by her personal history

In "Seventeen Questions About King Kong" (205–6), she acknowledges in the epigraph that her own claim to fame lies in one famous poet's assertion that she is the niece of King Kong. Nevertheless, she is more concerned about whether the King Kong story is "a myth? And if so, what does it tell us about ourselves?" She is most curious about the "anthropologist [who] always dream[s] animal dreams," wondering "must we?" The implication, of course, is that she's had similar dreams and is, perhaps, troubled by them, troubled by the way she sees the world beyond her own biases.

Cooper recognizes how much of the past is a confused jumble of false or misleading interpretations that necessarily cause one to question the way in which one has taken in volumes of information. In "Clementene" (207–8), she says of the poem's subject, "I always thought she was white," and within the same stanza notes that "there are so many things wrong with this story." Clementene was a seamstress who came "twice a year," whose "wishes were respected." It was a shock then to learn how "Clementene / died in our house a white woman and was claimed by her black daughter." To this reader, the poem is central to Cooper's struggle to resolve her feelings about family and their responses—as well as her own—to the "other" among them. She says as much in closing the poem: "Why, if I was not an accomplice, / did I feel—do I feel still—this complex shame?"

The final poem in the "Family Stories" section of *Green Notebook* is "How Can I Speak for Her?" (209–11). Cooper begins with the grandfather who loses his family to a yellow fever epidemic following Sherman's March through Atlanta leading to the end of the Civil War. Despite details that chronicle his life and his relations, she turns her focus to "an old black woman, a woman nobody knows" limping down the street. Cooper's grandfather is quite young when he observes this woman of "peculiarly deep, unmixed black color" and thus he perceives her in the same way he would have "had she been a chicken." The surprise for him, for Cooper and for the reader, comes when his grandmother, described generation after generation as a proud woman, approaches the stranger, traces the tribal scarifications on her dark face, and then, per Cooper's grandfather, "they embraced."

As with the first poem of "Family Stories," Cooper closes the section with a prose poem that unravels a lengthy long-ago family tale of what it means to be family, whether of blood relation or not. She reveals with great tenderness and poignancy the recognition between two women—one black, one white—who "met the gaze of the last person with whom she could converse." The use of the word "could" in this last phrase seems to sum up Cooper's frustration and delight at the manner in which the women—when one looks back on all of the poems in this section and of Cooper's oeuvre as a whole—reach or fail to reach out to each other, yet are able to speak in a language that "no one had heard her speak before" and so to make a kind of family in a world that constantly denies the union between us all.

LISA SPERBER

"I Could Not Tell You"
Green Notebook, Winter Road *and the Influence of Muriel Rukeyser*

Since the 1950s, Jane Cooper had wanted to shift toward poetry that could incorporate her social concerns. She had planned to publish an entire book oriented around World War II from a woman's perspective but finally judged many of those poems unsuccessful.[1] She felt her mode of writing would have to change; she wanted to write about other people and thought that, like her friend Grace Paley, she might have to turn to fiction to do so (Journal, February 1972, citing 1952–53).[2] In the mid-1970s, she wrote to her close friend Jean Valentine: "Have our poems mostly dealt with the personal, crises in relationships, loss? as opposed to Milosz's 'range' and moral authority?"[3] Cooper felt that her sense of history was important to her as an artist, and that she had "open[ed] out from the purely personal" in her essay "Nothing Has Been Used in the Manufacture of This Poetry That Could Have Been Used in the Manufacture of Bread" (1974), though she worried whether she would be able to do it again.[4]

Twenty years later, in 1994, *Green Notebook, Winter Road* draws extensively on this historical sensibility. In "Childhood in Jacksonville, Florida" she writes: "Oh I am the last member of the nineteenth century!" and in "The Past": "It seemed, when I was a child, as if you could just reach back and rummage in the 19th century" (197; 202). Cooper's sense of being on a historical precipice comes from a strong identification with her paternal family, who had immigrated to Florida from Spain three generations before: "I think now that one reason I didn't write more about my father's family earlier is that they seemed so powerful." While she honors her family, she also uses family to critically examine this Southern heritage: "I'm not using family background to create a domestic sense in this book—I'm using it to extend the individual consciousness through history and mythology."[5] Cooper's father, who became an interna-

tional expert on space aviation and law, and her uncle, the creator
of King Kong, were especially important figures:

> How have we come so far? How did we live through (in the
> persons, for me, of my father, of my uncle) radio, aviation, film,
> the conquest through exploration of Equatorial Africa, Persia,
> and Siam? My father thought the moon-walk silly, there were
> more promising worlds.
> And how do I connect in my own body—that is, through
> touch—the War of 1812 with the smart rocket nosing its way via
> CNN down a Baghdad street? How much can two arms hold?
>
> ("The Past," 202)

As for many Southern writers, Cooper's sense of being part of a
living history is also tied to the complex moral life of her family and
culture: "It's like being German. . . . Can any white person write
this, whose ancestors once kept slaves?" (203). While she interro-
gates her family's relation to race and class, her perspective is multi-
faceted: "Of course they were paternalistic. I honor their accom-
plishments. / What more have I ever done?" (204).

At the outset of *Green Notebook*'s "Family Stories" section, Coo-
per invokes Muriel Rukeyser and James Wright: "*Justice-keepers!
justice-keepers!*": "tell me how to redress the past, / how to relish yet
redress / my sensuous, precious, upper-class, / unjust white child's
past" ("Hotel de Dream," 189–190). *Green Notebook* includes an el-
egy to Rukeyser, "The Calling," and another poem that addresses
her directly. Cooper was first introduced to Rukeyser's work when
she was fourteen, when her sister brought Rukeyser's first two
books home from Vassar, giving the young Cooper a glimpse of a
living woman poet (109). Cooper and Rukeyser met at Sarah Law-
rence College in 1952 or '53, where they both taught, and were
friends for over twenty-five years until Rukeyser's death in 1980.
Cooper wrote a long foreword to the reissued publication of Ruke-
yser's *The Life of Poetry* (1949; 1996),[6] which theorizes the political
role of poetry in American life and consciousness. She also orga-
nized a symposium in honor of Rukeyser in 1979, resulting in a
daylong series of presentations by peers and former students, in-
cluding Alice Walker and Sharon Olds.[7]

Stylistically, Cooper is quite different from Rukeyser, who tends
toward an extroverted Whitmanic self-assuredness. She was, how-
ever, drawn toward the equally Whitmanic aspects of Rukeyser that

make her a poet of relation. In her foreword to *The Life of Poetry*, Cooper writes of poetry bringing us "face to face with our world" and ourselves "to a place where we sense the full value of the meaning of 'emotions and ideas in their relations with each other'"[8] (internal quote is Rukeyser). Cooper further describes "a sense of seeing farther than usual into the connections of things, and then of bringing intense pressure to bear on those connections, until they rise and fall into full consciousness for oneself and others."[9] Rukeyser's body of work is enormous, and her sense of political relations complex. In terms of her significance for Cooper's work, Rukeyser's commitment to social justice is especially important, including her poems on reconciliations, of self with self and self with other. Rukeyser's vision is evident in her poem "Despisals":

> Among our secrecies, not to despise our Jews
> (that is, ourselves) or our darkness, our blacks,
> or in our sexuality wherever it takes us
> [. . .] each like himself, like herself each.
> You are this.[10]

As a model of redressing race relations, Cooper would have been familiar with Rukeyser's "St. Roach" (1976):

> For that I never knew you, I only learned to dread you,
> for that I never touched you, they told me you are filth,
> they showed me by every action to despise your kind;
> [. . .] I could not tell you apart, one from another,
> for that in childhood I lived in places clear of you, . . .
>
> Yesterday I looked at one of you for the first time.
> You were lighter than the others in color, that was neither good
>   nor bad.
> I was really looking for the first time. . . . I reach, I touch, I begin
>   to know you.[11]

Racial segregation in the South was, of course, different from the Northern urban segregation about which Rukeyser writes, and in *Green Notebook*, Cooper describes a world in which blacks' and whites' lives were far more closely intertwined. Cooper insists that she does not "know" the characters about whom she writes, yet like Rukeyser, she works toward a better understanding of their experience and a less divided relationship with her own past. In "Clementene," about a mixed-race domestic worker who passed as white in the speaker's family home, Cooper invokes Rukeyser:

> I always thought she was white, I thought she was an Indian
> because of her high-bridged nose, coin-perfect profile
> where she sat in an upstairs window, turning sheets sides-to-the-
>   middle—
> There are so many things wrong with this story,
> Muriel, *I could not tell you*—
>
> (207)

One of Rukeyser's favorite assignments was to begin a poem with the phrase "I could not tell you," based on the belief that suppressed subject matter leads to our greatest revelations (254). Rukeyser is a double inspiration here: for uncovering suppressed material and for redressing race relations. Like Rukeyser's speaker in "St. Roach," this speaker tries to understand the ways in which racism distorts perception and uses observation as a tool to work toward a more accurate understanding; as Rukeyser wrote, "I was really looking for the first time." Rukeyser's exhortation, "No more masks! No more mythologies!" also comes to mind.

This commitment to uncovering suppressed relations is very much at work in Cooper's prose poem "Seventeen Questions About King Kong," written in response to her uncle Merian C. Cooper's 1933 hit film, which he cowrote, codirected, and coproduced. The poem is typical of "Family Stories" for the way in which it weaves together family history with political questions:

> Is it a myth? And if so, what does it tell us about ourselves?
>
> Is Kong a giant ape, or is he an African, beating his chest like a responsive gong?
>
> Fay Wray lies in the hand of Kong as in the hand of God the Destroyer. She gives the famous scream. Is the final conflict (as Merian C. Cooper maintained) really between man and the forces of nature, or is it a struggle for the soul and body of the white woman?
>
> (205)

The poem leads us toward a political interpretation of Kong as a representative African who evokes "the Dark Continent" and black sexuality, but Cooper's use of questions is more than a rhetorical pose; they allow her to consider the relationships between apparently disparate facts and experiences:

> When he was six his Confederate uncle gave him EXPLORATIONS AND ADVENTURES IN EQUATORIAL AFRICA by Paul du Chaillu, 1861. Does that island of prehistoric forms still rise somewhere off the coast of the Dark Continent, or is it lost in preconscious memory?
>
> Is fear of the dark the same as fear of sexuality? Mary Coldwell his mother would have destroyed herself had she not been bound by a thread to the wrist of her wakeful nurse. What nights theirs must have been!
>
> Why was I too first called after Mary (or Merian) Coldwell, till my mother, on the morning of the christening, decided it was a hard luck name?
>
> How does our rising terror at so much violence, as Kong drops the sailors one by one into the void or rips them with his fangs, resolve itself into shame at Kong's betrayal?
>
> Is Kong's violence justified, because he was in chains?
>
> Is King Kong our Christ?
>
> (205)

In the first quoted stanza, "prehistoric life forms" are associated with the "Dark Continent" through Du Chaillu. Because Cooper doesn't identify an owner of this "preconscious memory," however, it also becomes a general Western cultural myth. This unconscious, racialized fear of darkness is linked to a fear of hysterical female sexuality through Merian's mother, Mary Coldwell. Mary Coldwell's hysteria (and her daughter's correspondent fear of passing on Mary's name) transforms into "our rising terror at so much violence, as Kong drops the sailors. . . ." Merian's psychological relationship to gender and race becomes culturally representative; his terror becomes "our rising terror." The passage's final line, though rising out of associative logic, takes a sudden, surprising direction: "Is King Kong our Christ?" The fear of the abject other, which has produced Kong, finally becomes a full recognition of his persecution. This reversal of Kong's position revolves around recognizing the role he plays as a projection of cultural fears, desires, and need.

Throughout her life, Cooper tried to understand and write about her experiences in a larger social context. Rukeyser's emphasis on "really looking" and "seeing farther than usual into the connections between things" gave Cooper a method to explore her Southern roots, to bring into relation a range of people, facts, experiences, ideas, feelings, and myths. In *Green Notebook*, Cooper found the fruition she sought: "The real meaning of resurrection is to take up one's part in the world."[12]

Notes

1. Poems such as "For a Boy Born in Wartime," "P.O.W.," and "After the Bomb Tests" evidence her early political orientation.

2. Journal, February 1972, citing 1952–53, Berg Collection.

3. Ibid.

4. Ibid.

5. Ibid.

6. Muriel Rukeyser, *The Life of Poetry; with a New Introduction by Jane Cooper* (New York: First Paris Press Edition, 1996).

7. Alice Walker's essay, "*One* Child of One's Own: A Meaningful Digression within the Work(s)" [sic], appears in *In Search of Our Mothers' Gardens: Womanist Prose* (1967–1983).

8. Rukeyser, "Life of Poetry," xxi.

9. Ibid., xxvi.

10. Muriel Rukeyser, *The Collected Poems of Muriel Rukeyser* (New York: McGraw Hill, 1976), 137.

11. Ibid., 151.

12. Journals, 1979, n.d. month, Berg Collection.

MAGGIE ANDERSON

Moving toward Connectedness
Jane Cooper's "The Infusion Room"

"Poems are made in solitude," Jane Cooper wrote in the foreword to her collected poems, "but they move toward connectedness. Poetry calls me back to who I am; simultaneously, it releases me into a mode of being that is larger and more strenuous, in which the self is challenged only to be let up, a little changed" (21). For me, Cooper's poems have always seemed models of the effort of moving toward connection. Though she lived alone most of her life, she had a true and gracious gift for friendship. The epigraph to *The Flashboat: Poems Collected and Reclaimed* is from a letter from Emily Dickinson to Samuel Bowles—"My friends are my 'estate,'" and in reading through this volume, I am struck by how many of the poems are dedicated to, addressed to, or written about friends. Even the long, richly researched poems about Rosa Luxemburg, Georgia O'Keeffe, and Willa Cather are, among other things, records of intense personal engagement, of a kind of friendship with three women the poet never met but had come to know keenly and was challenged by.

One poem in particular, "The Infusion Room" (215–16), first published in *Green Notebook, Winter Road* (1994), mirrors the life of the poet in a somewhat unlikely community and also shows how poetry itself strives for connection. Here, Cooper puts her unwavering and accurate eye on a random group of people who are together solely because they all "have no gamma globulin." The deliberately cold, medical term, albeit alliterative and assonant, chafes against the facts of the body and its mortality; from the beginning, the stakes in this poem are high.

"The Infusion Room" is in two parts, with the first part structured as a litany, an intercessory prayer for the sick:

> Mercy on Maryanne who through a hole beneath her collarbone
> drinks the life-preserving fluid, while in her arm
> another IV tube drips something green. "It never affects me," she
> says, "I'm fortunate."

She has Crohn's and rheumatoid arthritis and osteoporosis, as well
    as no gamma globulin
as we all have no gamma globulin, or at least not enough.

By the fourth line it is clear that the speaker who asks mercy for others is herself one of the sufferers receiving her necessary dosage of the blood product that protects against a wide variety of immune deficiencies, the "life-preserving fluid." A camaraderie of shared experience develops in this group, and the poet evokes it in empathic detail. Cooper (it is clear that this poem is autobiographical) had been a sick child herself and so understands that fifteen-year-old Aaron who has missed a lot of school will "never quite make it up," however bright he is. As a member of this community, the poet is one with Paul, the cab driver who has sores on his ankles and whose work does not allow him to elevate his feet as the doctor has advised. His specific struggle reminds Cooper of her own luck: ". . . all those years of teaching at a college, the flexible hours, pleasant rooms / where you could always put your feet up if need be." She is also one with the used-Caddy salesman and the man who sells prostheses; with Mike, the pilot; and "the black kid strapped to his Walkman." Through identification, specificity, and what Cooper elsewhere refers to as "the sanity of observed detail" (118), the poem itself becomes an enactment of community, as she describes the bodies and the bits she knows of the lives of her companions.

The language of architecture and building often serve as central metaphors in Jane Cooper's poetry.[1] Here, it is significant that the shared space of this community is not a *ward*, or a *clinic*, or a *lab*, but a *room*, a homey place of refuge where comfort and even intimacy can be found.

"I was afraid this was just journalism," Jane told me when she first showed me this poem which I had lavishly praised. So I tried to work out what makes it so clearly different from a magazine feature story. Of course, there is the music—the repeated invocation, "Mercy on, mercy on," the long lines Cooper was known for loping through the poem's narrative, and the *effort* we cannot help but feel pressing on the words. At the end of the first section, the focus is on Maryanne and Aaron, "his huge sneakers" up on his mother's seat: ". . . she holds his hand lightly while he sleeps; / they look like the creation of Adam." The section ends with this transformation of a community "alert to real life" and "dense with ordinary detail" (174) into a work of religious art, echoing the prayer with which the poem opened.

Section 2 uses an entirely different voice that invites us—readers and outsiders—to stand back from the scene: "if you could see us now we'd resemble giant grasshoppers / whose skinny elbows vibrate slightly above their heads." Then the perspective shifts even farther away from the group to "a space ship" from which we can see the bodies on their black recliners as a busy harbor with cranes and "curious cargo." In the third stanza, we are moved back inside the room again, where "the TV twitters." We see the nurses "taking a break," a telling detail that reminds us of the medical situation and the community of what we now see as *patients*, receiving nothing less than their "daily habitable lives." Humor modulates the grim scene as the poet thinks: "We too could go on a talk show, / challenging truckers' wives, twins who have lost their Other," and then the poet is quietly unpeeling her sandwich and it is "almost time for the soaps."

Like others of Jane Cooper's poems that address her lifelong illnesses, this poem connects us to a somewhat elite community of sufferers, aristocrats of the unfortunate. In the prose piece "The Children's Ward," which follows "The Infusion Room" in *The Flashboat*, a ward of sick children (of which Cooper is one) turns into a spontaneous political movement as they try to get help for one of their own: "We had all called together to save Billy" (229). There is pride as well as urgency in this shouting; a seemingly defenseless group undertakes a united action and the conditions of their limited world are changed.

Throughout her life as a writer, Jane Cooper embraced this engaged aesthetic, as she worked in the intense but ephemeral writing communities of her thirty-seven years of teaching at Sarah Lawrence College and as, again and again, she called forth her many friends in her poems. "Poetry has been my community" (20), she wrote, and her unique gift was in advocating for engagement despite her own fears and physical weakness. A poet who was both unpretentious and ambitious, and as Donald Justice noted, unfailingly "interesting," Jane Cooper laid out the terms of her own calling in the title poem of her collected and reclaimed last book. In "The Flashboat" (144), she writes: "Room for only six – we will / all need to row." Though there is worry about her strength for this task—her "defective blood"—it is clear that she will not be alone in the boat. As a rope ladder is dropped over, the poet reaches for it and the move toward connection is complete.

Note

1. Viz. "The Builder of Houses, 35; "These High White Walls," 51; "Rent," 154; "The Blue Anchor," 157; and "The Children's Ward," 218, as well as "The Infusion Room" and the two book titles, *Maps & Windows* (1974) and *Scaffolding: Poems 1975–1983* (1984).

Hospital Time

On Illness and Caregiving in Jane Cooper's "The Children's Ward"

In her memoir, *The Virgin of Bennington,* Kathleen Norris writes that Jane Cooper credited Betty Kray, the well-known Academy of American Poets secretary who served as unofficial mentor and muse to many poets, with keeping her at work on an essay entitled "The Children's Ward." According to Cooper, Betty's urgings "brought me to the version I have. . . . [S]he chided me, and she made me write."[1]

Critics and poets have called "The Children's Ward," first published in *The Iowa Review's Collection of Contemporary Writing by Women* (1981) and later reprinted in *Green Notebook, Winter Road,* a long prose piece, and a short story. To me, it reads like a personal essay, which is not to say that poems and short stories can't traffic in the personal and autobiographical. As I began to write about "The Children's Ward," I wondered about this confusion of genre. Does it matter? Why has it been called a poem or a short story and not a personal essay? Was the voice too personal to be comfortable? Was it resistance to the essay, to memoir, to the confessionals, just honest confusion? Why do I care? Because to call it an autobiographical poem or short story or even "long prose piece" diminishes its hard painful truths about childhood illness, caregiving, the medical industrial complex, and the role that sickness can occupy in the psyches of the suffering.

In "The Children's Ward," we see a six-year-old Cooper navigating an unknown stomach ailment under the strict care of her Irish nanny, and later in the hospital with the kind Dr. Kerley and a staff of nurses who "never felt sorry for anyone," which was "what was so grand about them, they treated us just like ordinary children" (227). Cooper's parents and siblings are largely absent from the essay or exist as memories of a time before illness—they either can't engage with her or won't, and so Cooper recreates the rich world of the sick kid, which is largely one of solitude and caregiving by nannies and nurses. Of her parents, Cooper writes:

> My father blocked the light in the bedroom door. We stared at each other. Then the doorway was empty, he had left without saying anything. "He can't stand to see anybody sick," said my mother to my aunt, in a voice I wasn't supposed to catch. My aunt began to sing to me so my mother could go lie down. Far away the black freight train hooted. "She'll be comin' round the mountain when she comes," sang my aunt. (220–21)

There's so much in that stare between little girl and father, but what? A recognition on both of their parts that the father cannot bear to be present for his daughter's pain? Yes, but also the Depression Era's stoicism in the face of suffering and the gendered belief that it's mothers, aunts, grandmothers, and nannies who care for the sick, not men. The father can't say anything because he does not know what to say, and so the aunt comes to sing a song of distraction, which is also about movement, progress, and a fair bit of chance.

When Cooper and her mother take the train north to the hospital, a trip that takes "two nights and a day," she admits, "I would peer around at my mother. What should I talk to her about? For months I had been with almost no one but Nanny" (221). And it's Nanny—who is Irish but born in Scotland and who in church Jane watches pray for "her brothers and sisters at home, for her father who never made more than two pounds ten a week, and also for the young man she had come over to this country to meet" but couldn't bring herself to marry—that is the center of the first half of the essay (222). Cooper captures the day-to-day intimacies between caregivers and their charges. She admits, "God knew Nanny would have saved my life if she could, but since there was apparently no saving it, she did her duty" (219). This duty feels physical—Cooper sleeps with Nanny, watches her dress for church "under the tent of her white cotton nightgown," accompanies her to Catholic mass, and stares in awe at a first communion (221). Cooper loves the Bible stories Nanny tells her each night, but hates Abraham for killing his only son. Because of these stories and Nanny herself, Cooper learns to think of her illness in terms of guilt and penance. She remembers, "My sins were crying, lying, and not wanting to go to the bathroom," and after an accident when she wouldn't go, and "then I couldn't hold it any longer, shameful and brown it poured down my legs," Nanny "took the hairbrush to me" (222–23).

Nanny reminded me of another selfless Nanny, in the cartoon version of *Eloise*, entirely at service and without anything of her own except the church and discipline. I also thought of Charlotte Brontë's *Jane Eyre* and Jamaica Kincaid's *Lucy*, seminal texts that allow us to consider the liminal territory of caregiving. How generous of Cooper to give us so much of Nanny—and yet Nanny remains the childhood fantasy, the exotic mother substitute, the caregiver who cleans up the shit that the parents can't or won't. "The Cost of Caring," Rachel Aviv's 2016 *New Yorker* article[2] about mostly East Asian women who give up their lives with their own families to work as nannies in the United States so that they can send money back home, is a rare glimpse into the actual lives of caregivers and the sacrifices they make to care for other people's children. Emma, a college-educated mother of nine from the Philippines, takes a job as a nanny in Scarsdale because she knows she can put all nine of her daughters through college with this money, but trips home are almost impossible because of her visa status. After sixteen years of caring for American children and the elderly and interacting with her own children only on the telephone and through social media, Emma admits, "Sometimes I just want to throw up . . . it's just the same thing every day." What Aviv gives us as a journalist that Cooper can't as an essayist is the caregiver's voice and the interior world she inhabits. Cooper's choice is an intentional one and fitting for the historical moment in which she wrote it, but I couldn't help but think of Aviv's work as an extension of Brontë's, Cooper's, and Kincaid's. All four writers are engaged in the feminist project of trying to demystify caregiving through fleeting and not so fleeting glimpses into the lives of nannies and the children they both love and pretend to love for employment.

Cooper also demystifies the inner world of the child patient, and she's particularly adept at writing about the way in which childhood illness can distance children from their families and can make them wiser and sage-like at times. When the child enters the hospital, she detaches from the rituals and rhythms of family life and becomes part of what I call "hospital time" in an essay I published for the journal *Line Break* about my own childhood illness and hospital stay.

I was nine and away from home for the first time. There was a schedule, but I wasn't in on it. I started to understand the weird rhythm of doctors—the way they're never around when you need them or always with another patient or worst of all, in surgery. I went to appointments I didn't know I had, and always without my parents who were two hours away at their jobs. I began to cultivate irrational fears: *the orderly will lose me and I'll never see my parents again, the nurse will forget to tell my parents I'm having a brain scan and they'll leave without seeing me, or somehow my roommate and I will become separated and I'll have to sleep alone.*[3]

My anxiety was more acute than Cooper's, and yet she captures that same odd hospital life I came to understand as a new landscape, one that was first disorienting but eventually liberating. As painful as it may be, there's also freedom and power in leaving one's family behind and in learning to navigate and survive in a new world.

Cooper recreates this new world in vivid and mesmerizing detail. She writes of Dr. Kerley, the only adult to ever re-assure her: "From where I stood I could look directly into his blue eyes. . . . 'You know,' he said at once, 'you're going to be all right.' How could he understand all that I had felt? He told me before he told my mother" (226). She remembers her birthday on the ward and the nurses' gift to her of "a tiny wooden tea set with red trim," and that she "pretended [the cups] were overflowing with chocolate ice cream, cornflakes, and angel food" (227–28). Once a week, the children go to the roof to listen to stories, where "It was sunny and crisp on the roof, and as you stepped out of the elevator you could see a great sweep of sky, blocks of apartment buildings with a few trees down below" (228). It's in the ward too that a baby disappears from its crib one day, "Gone for an operation" the nurses claim, but the children know better.

One night, the children rally around when a small boy named Billy cries out in the night. Cooper describes the ward: "The whole place smelt like a zoo. There was the smell of fear, the warm animal smell of sleeping bodies, and the sharp stink of disinfectant coming up from the floors and the sheets" (229). As Billy cries for the nurse, the other children join in, and there's something powerful for Cooper in this moment of childhood solidarity. She admits, "But I couldn't sleep for a long time, thinking of how we had all called together to save Billy" (229). It's in the ward too that Cooper, as she learns how to eat again, falls in love with George, another patient who is getting better like Cooper. Her mother is shocked to find that she has "learned to talk just like George" and that it is "harelip language" (230). We sense that this new language is transgressive, and that it mirrors the way in which all writers learn to speak in multiple voices to tell their stories.

In the final paragraph of the essay, Cooper goes for a walk with her mother outside of the hospital. The two eventually come upon a school for deaf boys and stare "on ranks of boys in gray uniforms who marched and gestured rapidly with their hands" (230). Cooper's mother, overcome with a wave of emotion, explains the school to the young Jane, as her eyes "blurred with tears" (230). Cooper, pulling away from her mother and slipping "one hand out of its glove, experimentally" thinks, "But didn't she know we all had something?" (230) The subtlety of this ending is lovely and earned. Cooper will not become of one those institutionalized children, destined to never return to her family, and yet, she understands better than her mother ever will, that we all carry around some kernel of illness and trauma inside of us. There's something radical in this childhood knowledge and in the sage-like way the young Jane Cooper stares over "the curve of her mother's shoulder" to name us all as broken and sick.

As I read and re-read "The Children's Ward," I found myself thinking about a recent essay by Johanna Hedva in *Mask Magazine,* "Sick Woman Theory."[4] In this powerful and insightful essay, Hedva considers what protest means for the chronically ill and disabled, and she proposes a range of radical and emancipatory theories for re-thinking sickness, race, and the feminized body in both public and private spaces. Though Hedva calls herself "white passing," she allies herself with the Black Lives Matter movement and with women of color and transwomen in particular, whose bodies and stories are often ignored, abused, and pathologized in institutional settings. In the final section of her essay, Hedva urges us to reconsider our capitalistic relationship to care:

> The most anti-capitalist protest is to care for another and to care for yourself. To take on the historically feminized and therefore invisible practice of nursing, nurturing, caring. To take seriously each other's vulnerability and fragility and precarity, and to support it, honor it, empower it. To protect each other, to enact and

practice community. A radical kinship, an interdependent sociality, a politics of care.

Although Cooper's essay "The Children's Ward" precedes Hedva's by nearly forty years, I see in it an early gesture toward the new politics of care that Hedva argues for, one that is decidedly anti-capitalistic and emancipatory in its own private way. Cooper's radical project was an early attempt to make visible the "practice of nursing, nurturing, caring" and to take seriously her own childhood "vulnerability and fragility and precarity." This vulnerability is what makes the essay so readable and radical to this day. It asks us to consider some difficult questions: how can we better listen to the voices of patients, children, girls, and women, and how might we liberate caregivers and their charges? What does it mean to see one another in all of our bodily complexity? Which bodies get institutionalized and which are allowed to heal? And what if we're all broken?

Notes

1. Kathleen Norris, *The Virgin of Bennington* (New York: New York, 2001), 201.
2. Rachel Aviv, "The Cost of Caring," *The New Yorker* (April 11, 2016).
3. Carley Moore, "The Sick Book," *Line Break* (April 11, 2011).
4. Joanna Hedva, "Sick Woman Theory," *Mask Magazine* (January 2016).

KEVIN PRUFER AND PATRICIA YONGUE

"Vocation: A Life"

Poetry, we're told in school, is meant for interpretation. From our
first classroom encounters, we're instructed to read poems closely
two or three times, then dismantle them into their component
parts. Here is an example of imagery that suggests a larger emotion.
Here is a metaphor that makes specific what would otherwise be
empty abstraction. And here is a moment when the meter breaks, or
where the rhyme comes together in ways that seem, at first, less than
satisfactory. Why? What is the poet trying to *say* with her web of
symbols and similes?

Although such encounters might result in productive reading, to
approach a poem this way is, just as often, to do it a kind of disser-
vice. After all, one of the ways poems operate best is not through
telling us, in coded language, some larger meaning, nor do they al-
ways conceal their secret ideas behind layers of symbol, the poet
working in opposition to the reader. A great poem might play a
much larger game than this. Such a poem might not offer a hidden
conclusion, but suggest, instead, a fascinating mind at work on a
problem that is not solvable, that is not reduceable to paraphrase or
solution. What of the poem in which we sense, through the move-
ment of words, the employment of white space, the curious gram-
mar of the poetic line, the enactment of thought, the act of wres-
tling with a problem so large it cannot truly hold it, much less pin
it down?

Such is Jane Cooper's "Vocation: A Life." Reading this poem, it's
hard not to imagine Jane Cooper, in late middle age, looking back
over her life and wondering what the source of her poetry has
been . . . and what it has all added up to. These are enormous, un-
comfortable questions and, as such, they bring with them the qual-
ity of a reckoning—brought on, Cooper tells us in the "Notes"
section of *The Flashboat*, after a long engagement with the life's
work of another writer. "During one October spent in Iowa," she
explains, "I began to reread the works of Willa Cather. And it soon
became clear to me that whenever she wrote about the Southwest,

she was also writing about art." From the intersection of Cooper's own late-life reckoning and her engagement with the body of work of another woman writer comes this "Suite Based on Four Words by Willa Cather" that meditates intensely on the sources and uses of art—while also describing a writer trying to understand her own vocation through the work of another.

In diction and tone, "Vocation" is impossible to pin down neatly. Over thirteen pages, focusing on Willa Cather's Southwestern landscape scenes, it quotes extensively from Cather's work or alludes directly to it. At times, the poet looks into herself, finding affinities and similarities with Cather or coming to sudden realizations. Or, she interrogates Cather directly, offers a nearly academic interpretation of a scene, then makes observations about Cather's authorly intentions before seeming to slip into Cather's own consciousness. The effect, ultimately, is one of collage—though a collage unlike any other, in which the many pieces are composed of quotations, fictional characters, archival work, personal revelations, scholarly observations, and moments of mental telepathy.

Curiously, though, Cooper organizes the delicious, sometimes unruly components of "Vocation" into four seemingly neat categories, each apparently meant to delineate one perspective on artistic vocation: *Desire, Romance, Possession,* and *Unfurnishing.* Of course, there's something of the sleight of hand to this easy categorization; things are much more complicated than it implies. But that, too, is part of the fun of the poem.

The poem's architecture looks something like this:

Desire

"It begins in indolence / It begins as a secret intelligence rising like a tune" (237), Cooper tells us, alluding to Thea Kronborg's awakening among the ancient ruins of Panther Canyon in Cather's 1915 novel *The Song of the Lark.* In that novel, young Thea, an aspiring opera singer, takes a short break from the labors of her training to visit a rich suitor's Arizona ranch, where they spend several romantic days of, perhaps, erotic awakening.

For Cooper, the exercise of reading this scene has less to do with understanding the complexities of the characters involved and more to do with meditating on the intersection of sexual desire and transcendence as formative for artistic creation. Just as Coleridge finds the origin of art in Xanadu's "romantic chasm," in which a woman wails "for her demon lover," the earth "pants," and "a mighty fountain momently was forced," Cooper looks around Cather's Southwestern landscape and finds in it, ultimately, a vision of female sexual arousal in which Thea crouches naked in the bed of the stream and "the shards of ceremony glisten / from that bed / in a crack / of the world" (239).

But the desire here is not merely sexual, and it is certainly not merely earthy. Rather, it is transcendent and beyond words. "Everything," Cooper writes, "drops away / and is reborn as energy." Then, quoting Cather herself, she tells us "It has *nothing to do with words*," for the desire that begins art here—that thrusts Thea into her career as a singer and prompts Cooper to meditate on her own vocation—is wrapped up in the voiceless histories of those ancient women who preceded her, the people who "left no wounds in the earth," the ancient rock shelves holding the sun's heat "long after the canyon below has died into night," the vanished women recreated in her mind coiling clay into pots (237–38).

Here, artistic creation originates in the interaction between youthful sexual arousal and a larger experience of a humanity that has both died long before us and exists simultaneously in its own ruins (and in the spirit it has left behind and in herself). Ultimately, this takes the form of a transcendent, wordless erotic presence, which is found in the atmosphere of the ancient dead and the beyond-wordsness of sex—a desired, but unarticulable, *sense*.

Romance

If artistic vocation begins in wordlessness, it develops more volubly, from Eros into a desire for narrative, for story, for the imposition of the self onto the landscape. Here, Cooper shifts focus from Cather's *The Song of the Lark* to her short story "The Enchanted Bluff." For Cooper, this story (about the failed dreams of a group of men who, as boys, were inspired by stories of conquistadors in the Southwest) concerns both the paling of youthful ideals in the light of adult realities and larger questions of mortality and failure. The enchanted bluff itself is more frightening than wistful, "rear[ing] out of a homely, imagined desert / with all her dead on board" (240). The boys' vision is violent and doomed, and Coronado exists in the poem mostly as a figure whose dreams of discovery and immortality have resulted in failure. Cather herself plays an important part in this section, Cooper describing her early years through imagined scenes and actual quotations:

Who wrote by night for a dollar a column and studied by day
in your garish hat, in your too-thin coat
Imperious

Write ordinary life as though it were history
. . . so as to make us dream

But one must have simple tastes—to give up a good salary

What it must have cost you in your red-embroidered Liberty
gown
Throw all the furniture out of the window!

(240–41)

Of course, Cooper acknowledges, romance—fancy, story, delight, imagination—is central to artistic creation. We see this in the boys' delight at their tall tales and Cather's own vivid imagining of the Southwest ("Dreamer," Cooper addresses her, "you were almost forty / when you finally saw the Southwest"). But on the other side of our stories—our romances—is our annihilation, and that, too, is a force we write against. We invent stories so that we might preserve a bit of ourselves, and we bring them to people who will remember *us*.

To this end, Cooper alludes to two telling lines from Cather. The first, which comes at the beginning of the section, quotes from a pained letter she wrote to her friend Elizabeth Shepley Sergeant, in which she confessed to being afraid "of *dying in a cornfield*," forgotten and unfulfilled. The second comes at the end, a quotation from Cather's own translation of Virgil (from *My Ántonia*), asserting, "*for I shall be the first, if I live, / to bring the Muse into my country*" (241). Then, as a gentler romantic of counterpoint, Cooper closes the section with a vision of a very young Cather, "extravagantly reading / by the star of her railroadman's lantern / at an open window."

Possession

One of the ways we handle romance is by making property of it. Where earlier, Coronado inspired the children with flights of imagination, here he is possessed by Professor Godfrey St. Peter, of Cather's 1925 novel *The Professor's House.*

"THE PROFESSOR'S HOUSE," Cooper asserts, "is a novel about property," though her poem suggests that "property" is a very tricky word (243). St. Peter, for instance, makes property of the same Coronado the children fantasize about in "The Enchanted Bluff," zipping him into his enormous, multi-volume history of the conquistadors, his life's work and a subject he believes he is one of the world's great experts on. He treats the women around him and his deceased student Tom Outland similarly, luxuriating particularly in memories of Tom (Cooper suggests an unfulfilled homosexual relationship there and likens it to Cather's relationship with Isabelle McClung), keeping his diaries, retelling his story, and becoming unwillingly involved in struggles for ownership of the profits of his patents. "*If words . . . cost money,* he thinks, / they might taste this pure," Cooper wryly suggests, "The Professor as Coronado?" (243).

Professor St. Peter's ghost haunts this section, though Cooper often turns to address Cather directly, musing about the difference between *The Professor's House* being "most personal" (as Cather's companion Edith Lewis suggested) and Cooper's own assertion that it is "therefore not autobiographical," at least in any traditional sense: "unless the light comes from some faraway place / unless the source of light is beyond ourselves / unless we become ourselves / increasingly" (244).

In this way, Professor St. Peter makes a troubling figure for a meditation on artistic vocation. For artists—writers, poets—need to take possession (or come into ownership) of their characters, of stories, of the lives of others, which they then turn into art (or, as the previous section would have it, "romance"). But, Cooper allows, one finds a counterpoint to Professor St. Peter's version of possession in the story of his dead student, Tom Outland, whose journals (which form a centerpiece of the novel) concern his life-changing experiences in the ancient ruins of the Southwest. Here, Cooper describes him entering the mesa, solitary, looking out over the sunset and the falling snow,

. . . as the gold dies away
from his plundered birthright, to find it, after all, whole
and the arc of the evening sky whole
and the distant stars whole
as they have always been—till now?—he is at home
on earth, alone,
simplified

not possessing but
possessed.

(245)

If one troubling quality of artistic creation is the need to possess others, a less troubling quality is found here, in which the transcendent world possesses the writer, transporting him. For Cooper, possession is both violent and freeing. And both, simultaneously, are necessary for art.

Unfurnishing

Here, the extended metaphor of Cather's desert landscapes comes to an end where we probably predicted it might, in a meditation on mortality. The word *Unfurnishing* is inspired by Cather's brief essay on literary craft, "The Novel Démeublé," in which she argues that great writers (Tolstoi, Hawthorne) "present the scene by suggestion rather than enumeration"—that is, their settings "seem to exist not so much in the author's mind, as in the emotional penumbra of the characters themselves," beyond words and stripped down. Here, though, the idea of *Unfurnishing* becomes wrapped up in Cooper's thoughts about death and a refined sense of truthfulness that is acquired through artistic growth and knowledge of mortality:

> glimpse of a dooryard, glimpse of the South:
> *acacia*, with its *intense blue green* . . .
> *colour of old paper window-blinds*

touch and pass on

> The Archbishop forgives himself everything, even his
>   mistakes
> were no more than *accidents*. He is outside time

Poverty, solitude
have strangely flowered. And the Indian
will survive—

(248-49)

Death as both a motivation for and an end of vocation inhabits this
section, which looks back on earlier sections wistfully—"[Your]
secret? / It is every artist's secret. Your secret / was *passion*"—and med-
itates on Cather's own tombstone, on which is inscribed "THAT IS
HAPPINESS: TO BE DISSOLVED / INTO SOMETHING COMPLETE AND
GREAT." (Cooper, however, tellingly also offers us a nearly exact quo-
tation of the unetched lines that follow this in Cather's "My Ánto-
nia": "*When it comes, it comes / as naturally as sleep.*") Viewed from the
perspective of the distance of death and a life fully lived, the artistic
vocation itself defies summation:

When we try to sum up a lifetime, events cease to matter
just as, in the end, a novel's
plot does not matter
What we came away with was never written down
. . . . *The text is not there*—
but something was there, all the same, some intimacy . . .

(247)

Thus, what seemed at first to meditate on the sources of art, the
meaning of artistic vocation, on the difficulties of looking back over
life devoted to literature, becomes more intimate and ephemeral—a
reaching out toward an elusive, unapprehendable self. The poem
ends, paradoxically, on an image of morning in the desert:

supreme mirage of the flesh!

gold of a desert morning
light by which the writing
was composed

(249)

The desert, an enormously malleable image that has informed al-
most every moment of this poem, seems, at last, like the artistic
mind itself, filled with the light of inspiration and promise. But the
word "composed" is also weighted with all the complexity of the
rest of the poem—the difficulties of composing a life, questions of

the composure of the artist, and the certainty of the flesh's own eventual decomposition.

Ultimately, though, there's something unsatisfying about following the very path Jane Cooper lays out for us in this poem, from *Desire* to *Romance* to *Possession* to *Unfurnishing*. The poem is not nearly so neat as its architecture implies, nor as this essay suggests. At times, the sections seem not to progress but to be in conversation with each other, picking up later an idea that was dropped pages before, turning it over for a moment, then forgetting it again. Often, sections are connected by images, a window closing out one section only to open the next and recur in a third.

Moreover, it's hard not to find in the poem's progress the sense of the speaker herself changing, learning, aging. She begins assertively enough, offering a discussion of *The Song of the Lark*. Later, however, her discussions break down, Cooper intertwining them with glimpses of Cather's own life, glimpses that soon evolve into questions directed at Cather herself, melding, finally, with assertions that come from Cooper's own life. Finally, the poem moves into an intense sort of interiority, in which one line interrupts the next, in which the poem's many lyrical modes seem to slide uneasily into each other, suggesting not a clear discussion of the vocation of the artist (as in the first section) but a roiling mind that reaches into all sections of the poem at once.

And perhaps that's been the position of the poem all along—that what appeared like a clear-cut, organized lesson on vocation has always been a *reverie* in which we listen in on the thoughts of a highly intelligent writer whose own ideas, on the origins of art, on the nature of the artist, on the quality of vocation, deepen, intensify, and grow nuanced. There are no answers here. Things are not easily divided into subject headings and clarified. That was never the point, although it seemed once to be.

Instead, the point was to create, through the reflected light of another supremely talented writer, a complex meditation on artistic vocation. Or, in Cooper's own words, "poems are moments of the most acute consciousness. Through them, we reckon with the *now* and *here*, and yet we enter into a dialogue with history and otherness." The mind at work in such a poem is coherent without symmetry. It meditates fiercely but not necessarily linearly. It thinks hard, but any answers it produces come with revisions, alternatives, and contradictions.

BEATRIX GATES

Jane Cooper
Seventeen Names for Necessity

What matters earliest is a way of seeing: life is filmic—speech, changing light—pulsing in dynamic juxtaposition for Jane Cooper. She takes on her white, Southern histories; dream's power; and her own single, determined woman's life as part of "the fragile human settlement—" (157). Burning through, clear-eyed observation becomes her life-long teacher: "But to change one's images is like trying to revolutionize one's dreams. It can't be done overnight. Nor . . . effected by will. . . . Now I think you build it out of necessities—" ("Nothing Has Been Used in the Manufacture of This Poetry That Could Be Used in the Manufacture of Bread," 119).

"Seventeen Names for Necessity" offers a vision of Jane Cooper's complex, changing resolve towards how she would meet the world responsibly in her poetry.

1. Jane Cooper's poems define passion, and the first bright passion is survival. Not that love or sex do not matter—strong shaping life occurs in poems, such as "Eve" and "Obligations." But to speak of survival first is to enter questions of necessity and what is important. Since Jane Cooper was not supposed to live past the age of seven, she comes to her impassioned questioning partly through a heightened sense of her life possibilities and the lens of illness. As a five- and six-year-old, Cooper takes in her situation and the weight of what the adults say or don't say in "'The Children's Ward."

2. *How* to survive was a passionate, dogged, day-by-day question. Isolation, as a companion to illness, focused Cooper's principled doubt and tense resolve, including the choice to be ruthlessly fair-minded, beginning in childhood. Carving out a space for herself, Cooper imagines more for her life: for love, for the life of the mind reaching toward the world and yearning to be part of it! "The Children's Ward" ends cannily with Jane's question for her mother, "But

didn't she know we all had something?" (230). Cooper's nervy question explodes her youthful isolation; she joins in without fuss or approval. This early knowledge of everyone having "something" becomes the world of the poem, born to Cooper and carefully constructed to share meaning as seeker, questioner.

3. Jane Cooper is the young writer who absorbs everything and protects this information within the structure, space, and, later, the very motion of air in the poem. Resisting falsity is crucial, as she wakes to grief, all senses open in "Iron":

> . . . and the taste of fresh blood
> like iron against my tongue.
>
> . . . .
> I think some nerve is exposed—
> . . . .
> or a fine skin was peeled off
> the night you were killed.
>
> Conversations at breakfast
> have the stripped truth of poems.
>
> (55)

Unafraid to explore contradiction or enter the dream, she renames the light of altered perception, "all our darkness tears / With meanings" and enters *our* century's burden in "After the Bomb Tests" (88).

4. Awareness of the value of this journey takes time, as Cooper "leav[es] behind a breath of loves and angers" ("March," 71). Cooper discovers fidelity to the mind, deciding anger and the powerful senses. In early love poems, anger demands authenticity, which may not include traditional marriage or children. Urgent relation to the world evolves from camaraderie and friendship among women committed to truth-telling (119). A lover offers little understanding of Cooper's critical metaphors of war and gender in "The dark home of our polarities" (94). Disappointment is raw in "Twins" (85): "You pray / For marriage as another man might pray / For sleep after surgery, failing / More ether . . ."

5. "The Knowledge That Comes through Experience" dryly suggests with emphatic half-rhymes that a woman noncombatant who

has been consumed by love and war may need to be dead to be recognized. Even curiosity is mocked:

> . . .There is much to learn
> And curiosity riddles our rewards.
> It seems to me I may be capable,
> Once I'm a skeleton, of love and wars.

(86)

Anger is useful in protecting how she will live and work. "Coda" ends "March" by appraising reciprocity: "Everything has been offered, nothing given. / Everything, not the first thing has been said" (71). But faith in the act of writing will bridge the dilemma, alive for the next writer to wrestle with: "After me who will sit here, patiently writing?" Cooper reframes commitment to interior space, refuses to give up her purpose. If the early love poems portray an ambivalence masking anger, they move through the world seriously, confronting the destabilizing effects of war on love, and Cooper's own fierce desire for autonomy.

6. In "Waiting," after feelings of shame and release from expectation come essential questions. Cooper calls herself into being:

> My body knows it will never bear children.
> . . . .
>
> Old body, old friend,
> why are you so unforgiving?
>
> . . . .
>
> Let compassion breathe in and out of you,
> breathe in and out of you

(140)

7. For Cooper, forgiving means valuing her experience. Telling is a kind of forgiving: "My whole intention as a writer had changed. . . . I set aside the kind of anger that often goes along with sexuality, one of the pivots of my work" (121). Questioning holds, the rest drops away. She comes to terms with what a sense of truth might be in the world. "The Faithful" names emotional complexity, asking, "Why should I grieve after ten years of grieving?" (28). The very shape of imagination transforms loss:

What if last night I was the one who lay dead
While the dead burned beside me
Trembling with passionate pity
At my blameless life and shaking its flamelike head?

A call to living is made by the late beloved—"its flamelike head,"—
and compassion is alive. Life lived is "blameless." Death is known,
love too, as loss; thus, the poet's deep dream demands reinventing
sincere terms for living and commitment to the toll of experience.
In "Inheritances," the last section of "Dispossessions," Cooper
chooses Rilke to confirm: "And: *Still it is not enough / to have memo-
ries, they / must turn to blood inside you*" (134).

8. In "Family Stories," the evolution of childhood experience be-
comes utterance as real as Rilke's *blood* (134). Sharing startling sto-
ries, Cooper witnesses the "'complex shame' of a white Southern
heritage" (Foreword, 20) in textured poet's prose. In "Class," from
"Family Stories," *How* marks action and is the first word of each
stanza in Cooper's cinematic memory:

How the shrimp fisherman's daughter did a handstand . . .
proving she owned no drawers
    just as my grandmother's old black Packard drove up like a hearse
                                                                (200)

The daughter is her own actor, as is the girl narrator, who anticipates
doom from the eyes inside her grandmother's car. Her own relation-
ship to her grandmother's judgment, final as death, is dread. The story
illustrates assumptions of propriety and wealth against stories readily
understood by the young as wounding. This fable invites us in, not
without humor. The girl's perspective highlights divisions the adults
ignore and perpetuate. "Class" delivers the hypocrisies without orna-
ment and with emphatic lack of end line punctuation.

9. "Ordinary Detail" tracks the nightmare edge of the possible, a
rupture common in our time:

I'm trying to write a poem that will alert me to my real life,
a poem written in the natural speech of the breakfast table,
of a girl spooning yogurt . . .
                                                                (174)

Cooper sets out the comprehending vision, inhabited by a girl who is at the beginning of her journey, and then questions the dream:

And yet this poem must allow for the unseen.
Last night, the girl dreamed of a triple-locked door
at the head of a short flight of steps. Why couldn't she get in?

(174)

Accessible, inaccessible; the need to enter the dream, the door must be hers. The questions are natural to the girl, primary to the poet. The governing voice of the imaginer will deduce no easy answer—but bring the weight of her questions to life.

The question she must answer: "How to take possession of that room?" She returns to a present without conclusion, "Remembering, she loses track of her sentence . . ." as if erasing causality, while remembering the shape of her life. The muted, destructive atmosphere demands more of us, and the girl, faithful to her experience, knows it: "The girl is walking furiously, under a mild, polluted sky." Cooper details an anger that will teach and perhaps preserve the girl.

10. There's a turning in "Family Stories" where Cooper explores the right to claim subject matter as well as the space to claim prose in "How Can I Speak for Her?" (209). A beautifully complex narrative unfolds as the two women—an African woman, once a slave, and Cooper's great-grandmother, once her mistress—are envisioned by Cooper's grandfather. Ultimately, it is language that binds the women and the little boy together. Cooper focuses on the powerful moments of discovery:

What my grandfather remembered, all those many years later, was that she called out in a language none of them knew she knew, a language no one had heard her speak before, from so deep in her throat it was as if she coughed up stones. That she flew down the steps to stop just short of the African in the dust. That slowly then, as if unsure, she just traced the scarifications graved like a cat's face into the African face. That each met the gaze of the last person with whom she could converse. That—but how can I speak for her, whose name would again be lost? —they embraced. (211)

The slowing of incident extends through each specific action. Cooper makes sound carry the utterance between the African and the great-grandmother, astonishing with, "it was as if she coughed up stones." To dramatize the sequence, "Which" rises from memory to compel action, and the charge moves inside the unspoken, and perhaps unspeakable years, shared in the lives of slave and slaveholder. The poet navigates the ending by bringing attention first to the nameless African woman and then asserting the two women's present. She asks the challenging question as poet/teller: "—but how can I speak for her, *whose name would be again be lost?*—" My italics show the poet's awareness of naming-without-naming the African woman, acknowledging the woman's centrality in the history, many times untold and unknown. To place this question before "they embraced" alters the force of the story; it is the untold we feel most strongly in this journey across time.

11. Cooper's cinematic eye records a questioning of herself, white Southerner observing a moment freighted by the frights of slavery. The investigation of the unlikely bond occurs through the first language of the African and the grandmother's knowledge of the language (learned of necessity and shared by the two women). The story needs the chase of prose across the page—and using a poet's timed hesitations in dashes to pitch the drama helps realize the story. Perhaps the only way for her to tell it was to walk through it, while hearing the sound of "stones coughed up." The utterance unblocks the fearsome connection.

12. Another question of conscience interrupts "Praise": "Is this enough—when I love our poor sister earth?" (156). She asserts: "Nothing is enough!" while placing her own survival in a question at the end: "who could have foretold / I would live to write at fifty?" This identifies awareness of her "survival . . . as an art of the unexpected" (122). So Jane Cooper names her necessities: poetry is an "*action against fear*" (134).

13. Like "Praise," "The Blue Anchor" holds tenaciously to the demands of "the fragile human settlement" (157). The beginning implies release, possibly death:

The future weighs down on me
just like a wall of light!

All these years
I've lived by necessity.

The groundwork laid out, the poet does not ask but throws down
the challenge:

To live in the future
like a survivor!

Embracing vulnerability and responsibility, she ends:

—never forgetting
the wingprint of the mountain
over the fragile human settlement—

The element of air—flight, mind, wonder—falls through the earth.
The monumental become smaller and the temporal rises. The dash
gives promise to unknowing, while the first words, "—never forget-
ting," call us home.

14. It's no accident that "Threads: Rosa Luxemburg From Prison"
follows "Praise" and "The Blue Anchor" in *The Flashboat*. When
Cooper decided to enter the imagination of Rosa Luxemburg
through her letters, she found a unique form of witness that juxta-
posed narrative and lyric. In personifying structures of understand-
ing, Cooper chooses her subjects, marked by "the same urgency to
explore a woman's consciousness. . . ."[1] In "Threads," Luxemburg's
daily awareness is fresh, remarkable: "Suppose I am really / not a
human being at all but some bird or beast? / I walk up and down
my scrap of prison garden— / . . . the grass is humming with
bees—" (159). Luxemburg's consciousness elicits wonder, transcen-
dent in the midst of bereavement, love and war. Far from sentimen-
tal, the voice continues, "Still, nature is cruel, not a refuge." The long
poem required creating a profound, resonant spirit from the com-
passion evident in the prison correspondence with Sophie Lieb-
knecht, wife of Luxemburg's co-revolutionary Karl Liebknecht,
and Cooper's lyric intensity is stark and bold within the framework.
To bring us Rosa Luxemburg—with her radical environmental
consciousness and loving vision—is a challenge ripe for Jane Coo-
per's engaged vision.

The exacting doubt coupled with confident passion in Cooper's earlier poems helped bring her to Luxemburg's life. Rosa Luxemburg bears her imprisonment at incalculable cost as the vicissitudes and desperate cruelty of World War I swirl around her and, in the end, take her. In "Threads," we feel the loving, indomitable pulse of inner life and deep breath of Cooper as hearer and seer. "The source of love is the first care of a humane politics . . . for each of us, momentary to be celebrated."[2] Listen to the second stanza in "2. Breslau—November–December, 1917," addressed to Sophie Liebknecht, as a vibrant conditional "you":

> If only I could send you
> like a starry cloak
> the confident joy I feel. I lie awake
> in black wrappings of boredom, unfreedom and cold.
> A distant train hoots. Now there's the squeak
> of damp gravel under the desolate boot
> of the midnight guard, who coughs. It becomes a song.
>
> (161)

The poem is able to imagine the guard's boot becomes "a song" as desolate as imprisonment. There are deep questions for Cooper that emerge from the cell of Rosa Luxemburg. It is the whole body imagining: "My cell trembles . . . / . . . Life itself, / the riddle, becomes the key to the riddle" (162). The poem does not question "Life itself"; it is given, a trembling *of* life.

15. Cooper aligns herself with the word "heroic" to transmit the need for transformation felt by Luxemburg: "Even this war, / this huge asylum, this casual misery / in which we drown, this too must be transformed / into something meant, heroic" (162). Cooper has transformed "heroic" in her own lexicon. Remember the sense in "Nothing Has Been Used . . ." that writing "a book of war poems from a woman's point of view" (102–3) required a "heroic" stance. "Threads: Rosa Luxemburg from Prison" achieves a marriage of history and the interior. Cooper had hoped: "I would write as a noncombatant, a witness" envisioning a significant stance for her poems (101). Cooper presciently asked, "what happens to peasants in a war? ('Women go / On sweeping out the house where they were killed'), while exploring the state of mind of the wisest human beings . . . which I saw as a kind of recovered innocence, knowledge, tempered by extremes of mental and physical suffering" (105).

This "recovered knowledge" could be Rosa Luxemburg's, written from her cell. Jane Cooper is the poet and person who recovers the soul of that knowledge. When Cooper talks about "the necessity for changing myself, for finding a new style both of being and writing, to go with the changed realities I now perceived" (119) in this essay, she could be speaking to "Threads." Because this poem, a call from inside a history and a life, demands to be heard personally as a plea for "This lovely world!" (165). It takes a visionary to teach us, when faced with no evidence of love. Jane Cooper serves the forms of praise and grief faithfully. Jane Cooper is the person who can imagine what it is to reach toward transformation of consciousness through the lessons of a woman's lifebody.

16. Cooper allies with Rosa Luxemburg's imagination—she who decides to be open to wonder—as her life is dismantled by war. Doubt and questioning, a need to engage with the world and with love, develop into a profound statement of passion for life on this earth in "Threads." Cooper asks *us* to wonder if we can possibly do the same. What does she tell us about ourselves, our necessities? Must we dream our questions? Her images will bring news and our own history will question us.

17. Cooper looked at her complex Southern past in her writing by weighting the accuracy of who is visible and how. The sign of a real ally is a witness, unafraid of the truth, who does not need to make herself the subject. "Threads" captures spare truthfulness. Luxemburg's experience, brilliantly lit from inside her cell's confinement, "one with your pain, your helplessness, your longing/one with you in my helplessness" is a lyric of despair and studied tenderness (164). This is Jane Cooper's gift: intimate connection that radiates outwards: "Thus passing out of my cell in all directions / are fine threads connecting me / with thousands of birds and beasts / . . . beyond even / the radiant skin / of the globe" (167).

Notes

1. Jane Cooper, Foreword, *Scaffolding, New and Selected Poems* (London: Anvil Press Poetry Ltd, 1984), vii.
2. Ibid., viii.

CELIA BLAND

Ordinary Details
Humor in the Work of Jane Cooper

Like many artists who suffered an extended childhood illness, Jane
Cooper had the mischievous humor of the kid who got away with
things. Cooper's gimlet eye lingers over what Anne Carson calls
"error—and its emotions." Critique punctuates her work like those
delicate "wing print[s] of the mountain" in "The Blue Anchor"
(157). This is not to say that her poems *merely* laugh; they also exam-
ine, regret, and delve into what Kazim Ali, in an essay on her work,
called a "far-ranging concern with sound and open spaces in the
language." Certainly, however, Cooper's poetry serves as an observa-
tory for human frailties as she deflates her own and others' unthink-
ing adherence to the puffed-up prejudices of class, sexuality, race,
and culture. What she discovers in the ordinary details of life—"the
natural speech of the breakfast table" ("Ordinary Detail," 174)—is a
wry tolerance for others and even, ultimately, for herself.

I am advancing an argument for Jane Cooper the humorist or, at
the very least, the humorous (her middle name *was* "Marvel," after
all). I posit that the family and friends who appear in her later po-
ems and essays are akin in eccentricities, virtues, and faults to Jane
Austen's gentry. There is Cooper's father, the air space lawyer, who
works out in billable hours "the legal limits of the upper air" and
opines that the circumference of the earth "was too small for intel-
ligent aircraft design or navigation" ("From the Journal Concern-
ing My Father," 196); there is her uncle, anthropologist Merian C.
Cooper, director of *King Kong*, who chose "to play the [pilot] who
over and over exult[s] to shoot Kong down." ("Seventeen Ques-
tions About King Kong," 206). She even created herself as a charac-
ter in family comedies: the young Jane, pooping on the floor and
spanked with a hairbrush by her Scottish nanny; sickly Jane who
overhears an adult comment that she, in her childish Sunday best,
looks "like a picked chicken" (225); or adult Jane who exults "Oh"
(that Victorian *"Oh"!):*

Oh I am the last member of the nineteenth century!
And my excitement about sex, which was not of today,
is diffusing itself in generosity of mind.

For my mind is relaxing its grip, and a fume
of antique telephones, keys, fountain pens, torn roadmaps,
old stories of the way Nan Powell died
(*poor girl!*) rises in the air
detached but accurate—
almost as accurate
as if I'd invented them.

("Childhood in Jacksonville, Florida," 197)

This world of torn roadmaps and gossip about *poor* Nan Powell
is peopled with such characters (in the Southern sense of the
word—*char-act-ters*) as Wanda, Clementene, and Cora Crane, Ste-
phen Crane's mistress, who ran a Jacksonville cathouse and chatted
affably about bloodlines with Cooper's aunt at a dog show. Humor
appears in the juxtapositions of details, in the mocking *oh!'s* of par-
entheticals, in the long view of a girl, "shackled-with-politeness"
("Nothing I Meant To Keep," 183), who becomes a woman like
"that famous wooden music hall in Troy, New York, / waiting to be
torn down / where the orchestras love to play" ("Waiting," 140).

Telling stories of her own and others' haplessness, Cooper exhib-
its an amused understanding of the foibles and strictures of polite
society. There are thunderous farts; "touching" oneself—"'if you
don't stop . . . we'll have to take you to the hospital and get it cut
off'" ("The Children's Ward," 223); "King Kong slavering at the
window" ("Mary Coldwell," 191); and a cousin eagerly lecturing
about the two-inch landscapes she has painted on cobwebs ("Hobby
Lobby," 198). Always a stubborn integrity, a subtle understanding,
and an exacting, even sly, wit. Consider the self-deprecating moder-
nity of such titles as: "Dream in Which the Routine Quality of My
Imagination Is Fully Exposed"; the aforementioned "Nothing Has
Been Used in the Manufacture of This Poetry That Could Have
Been Used in the Manufacture of Bread"; the mentioning of her
great-grandfather, "head of the Southern Masonic Female College"
("How Can I Speak for Her?," 209); and her response to her profes-
sor in "a poem with capital letters" (written all in lower case):

john berryman asked me to write a poem about roosters.
elizabeth bishop, he said, once wrote a poem about roosters.

do your poems use capital letters? he asked. *like god?*
i said. *god no,* he said, *like princeton!* i said,
god preserve me if I ever write a poem about princeton . . .

(82)

(One can imagine Cooper's soft guffaw as she wrote: *god preserve me!*)

Cooper's poems are funny because of what they include—the absurdity of the author of *Dreamsongs* advocating Elizabeth Bishop's roosters (Bishop representing the "appropriate" model for an aspiring female poet)—and because of what is *missing,* as in a slapstick moment from "Class":

How the shrimp fisherman's daughter did a handstand against the
    schoolyard fence
proving she owned no drawers
just as my grandmother's old black Packard drove up like a
    hearse . . .

(200)

Perhaps Cooper's humor, incisive as it is, is rooted in her own initial humility, even insecurity, about her work—or at least in her internalization of the world's judgment of that work. Early reviewers critiqued her poetry as too mannerly, and Cooper, in her early thirties, may have been her own harshest critic, secreting poems she couldn't, at that time in her life, "face out" or bear because the implications of "the full range of intuition" in her work reflected a woman she didn't want to be. Adrift in unhappy love affairs in a post-war world where women poets were "a contradiction in terms," she not only put away poems that critiqued a misogynist world but she forgot them entirely ("Nothing," 108).

This impulse to suppress is the opposite of the "generosity of mind" ("Childhood in Jacksonville," 197) and the "radiance of attention" ("Rent," 154) that were her greatest poetic desire and ambition. Suppression and repression were impulses encouraged, even enforced, by the brilliant and drunken company of male poets, her peers. The negative consequences of seeing and speaking were so prevalent and so destructive that, in an aphorism Cooper quotes from Anaïs Nin, "In order to create without destroying, I nearly destroyed myself" ("Nothing," 117). In the early 1950s, in one of these censored poems, she asserts:

The urge to tell the truth
Strips sensuality
Like bark stripped from the tree.

("The Urge to Tell the Truth," 84)

—as if allowing herself the truth of her own vision would ruin any chance she had for a conventional life of love, marriage, and family. To be a poet, it seemed, she must choose a singular life.

Cooper's frequent illnesses certainly contributed to her "other" viewpoint. She was critical, eagle-eyed at a time when the feminine ideal demanded nurturance and self-sacrifice. Adrienne Rich decried women poets' "niceness" ("Nothing," 112) as a form of institutionalized cultural repression, and Berryman's Henry opines, "them lady poets must not marry, pal"—they are castrating, immodest, unnatural. Granted, the force and clarity of Cooper's voice is everywhere in her poetry's acuity, its concern with big unanswerable questions, in poems about artists and activists (Rosa Luxemburg, Emily Dickinson, Willa Cather, etc.), but readers will also find in the work of the 1950s and '60s a grade-school correctness and modesty, the consequences of which damage her poetic "gift for seeing afar and seeing through" ("Nothing," 115).

Cooper's assessment of her own work has been discussed by Jan Heller Levi. Cooper called herself a "minor" poet (that is, *occasional, modest*, like those Elizabethans quoted in Barbara Pym novels). The epigraph for her poem "Seventeen Questions About King Kong" tenders a troubling judgment by poet James Wright: "The most amazing thing I know about Jane Cooper is that she's the niece of King Kong" (205). By including this as an epigraph (I almost wrote *epitaph*), Cooper "tells on" herself and on Wright—as if neither of them could make grandiose claims for Cooper as artist. It's an odd gesture.[1] One can't imagine, for instance, Robert Lowell conceding that the most interesting thing about him was his marriage to Jean Stafford or to Elizabeth Hardwick. Cooper's wit travels true as a well-shot arrow—*no hyperbole has been used in the manufacture of this verse*—but perhaps it occasionally hit too near her own artistic ego.

In the 1950s, she later wrote, "I . . . put [poetry] to one side, precisely because I still hoped [for marriage and children]. . . . I seemed to have made a mess of my most intimate friendships, and poetry . . . now looked less like a source of renewal . . . than the housewrecker" ("Nothing," 115). It is only after the publication of these suppressed poems in "*Mercator's World*" in 1974 that her work begins to resonate with vulnerability and an enjoyment of the ridiculous. In my view, the result of this reclamation was the redemptive generosity of absurdity. By acknowledging the poems of "*Mercator's World*," Cooper stood symbolically behind work she no longer "inhabited," signaling a shift away from perfectionism and towards ambivalence, complexity, and disappointment. In so doing, she opened the door to the "scherzi" of playful jests and joyous moments ("Nothing," 105).

The connection forged between the serious and the serio-comic is Cooper's enduring theme: it is key to her survival as woman, as artist. In the "flashboat" of her work, she both "relish[es] yet redress[es] / my sensuous, precious, upper-class, / unjust white child's past" ("Hotel de Dream," 190).We hear the sibilant protest of "*Still it is not enough / to have memories, they / must turn to inside you*" as she rehearses the guilty tales of her Southern childhood ("Dispossessions," 134). In these family poems, as in the poems about her illness, she sought to

connect in my own body—that is, through touch—the War of 1812 with the smart rocket nosing its way via CNN down a Baghdad Street[.] How much can two arms hold? How soon will my body, which already spans a couple of centuries, become almost transparent and begin to shiver apart?

("The Past," 202)

Her concern for inheritance—what would she leave behind for her beloved students, her peers, her readers before "shivering apart"—prompts Cooper to delve into the details of worlds forsaken or lost. How to breech the morality of memory and forgiveness—'I want to forgive / what was never done to me / outright"—so as to justify the necessity for action, for particularities of grammar and punctuation and vocabulary, as they would play out in the next generations of poets, particularly poets of the "lowercase" persuasion ("After the Blackout," 127)?

We who are Jane Cooper's inheritors need—*another necessity!*—to reread the work of this woman recently memorialized as "virginal," who wrote passionately of her love affairs; this woman regarded as staid and decorous, who was inspired so often by the chaotic truth of dreams; and this writer who described the past with a serio-comic sagacity that is kissing cousin to the succinct tragedy of illness, guilt, and frustration. She offered, for those who dig deep enough, the hard won hope of the bloodroot, "releasing its unhurried freshness, / half earth, half air" (the blossom of that "contradiction in terms" of woman poets) ("Bloodroot," 184; "Nothing," 108).

"For," she concluded, "If my poems have always been about survival—and I believe they have been—then survival too keeps revealing itself as an art of the unexpected." Which may include those moments when a demure silence is broken by unexpected—even raucous—laughter ("Nothing," 122).

Note

1. And a misleading one as well. Wright was a beloved friend and devoted supporter of her work.

PAMELA ALEXANDER

A Boat to See by, a Life to Row

While *The Flashboat* gathers Jane Cooper's poetry from 1954 to 1999 under one cover, it is not a conventional volume of collected work. For one thing, the poems have been rearranged to show the order in which they were written. The change from the earlier order can be dramatic: the poem "The Flashboat" opens *Scaffolding* rather than ends it, for instance, and in *Maps & Windows* the entire section called "Mercator's World" has been moved from last to first. Knowing this offers insight into the writer's process: in some books, later work led us to earlier, so that their re-arrangement talks to us (we now see) about origins.

Another unusual feature is that this book includes eighteen "new" poems (previously unpublished or unpublished in book form). Since they appear throughout, according to the chronological plan, *The Flashboat* is not "collected and new" but (true to its subtitle) "collected and reclaimed." It makes sense that poems set aside because they didn't fit earlier books can now find a place in the broader context of forty-five years of work. There is a wholeness, a humanity, about *The Flashboat* that is different from the wholeness of the books it includes: they were constructed, while this book shows us something of how it was that the wholeness was accumulated, earned, lived, won.

For these structural reasons, the book gives a palpable sense of the writer at work. This will be of interest not only to scholars and fellow writers but also to general readers who care about the process by which poems get made. It's an uncommon occasion in the greater world of letters that a writer's material is provided straight from her desktop, so to speak; but Cooper has always been uncommonly open about how she works. Her 1974 essay "Nothing Has Been Used in the Manufacture of This Poetry That Could Have Been Used in the Manufacture of Bread" (included in *The Flashboat*) is an extraordinarily clear-eyed meditation on the development of her work, as well as on the larger social and political context of the times. She began writing in a world reeling from two global conflicts. World War II, of course, obsessed her, but as subject matter it posed difficulties because she was not a direct participant. And women were also marginalized in more insidious ways. It is fascinating to see how inner and outer circumstances interact.

The essay is already quite well known, so I will not dwell on it here but only point out that its stance is oddly both autobiographical and not. "[P]oetry isn't autobiography," Cooper says. "Autobiography is not true enough; it has to be rearranged to release its full meaning. . . . A poem uses everything we know."

Poetry is what Jane Cooper is about, what she has worked at patiently and passionately. When she says, in the brief but compelling introduction to *The Flashboat,* "Poetry has been my community," the work that follows makes it clear she is not talking exclusively about poets, friends, or even living people. There is community in this poetry with artists of all kinds, from the contemporary painter Shirley Eliason to Emily Dickinson and Theodore Roethke. While there's a long tradition of writing to or about other artists, Cooper contributes to it with a calm intensity that reawakens us to the necessity within the tradition. And she does so without sounding especially "traditional."

Seeing oneself as a member of a community, as someone taking part in the long story of literature, requires the ability to make connections to others. Empathy is one of the foremost characteristics of *The Flashboat* (sentimentality is not), and I'd like to focus on the way it sometimes fuses content and technique. There are moments throughout the book in which poems momentarily blur the boundaries between people. This sounds romantic, and indeed "The Racetrack" section of "Acceptances" contains the line "So we were one before we spoke or kissed." But far more often the deep connection between people that the strategy invokes is about something other than the romantic. It may be, nevertheless, about love.

A couple of examples, then. "For My Mother in Her First Illness, from a Window Overlooking Notre Dame" opens this way:

Why can I never when I think about it
See your face tender under the tasseled light
Above a book held in your stubby fingers?
Or catch your tumbling gamecock angers?
. . . .
But I must reconstruct you, feature by feature . . .

The poem proceeds to that reconstruction, from the mother's "sailor's gaze" to her "Gothic nose." The third stanza (of four) reaches for the personality that wore the face.

> Arrogant as a cathedral or the sea
> You carry your blue space high and quick
> On a young step, tapping or chivalrous.
> Pilgrim of the ridiculous
> And of a beauty now almost archaic,
> I miss your swift inward, your needle's eye.

And then, at the end of the poem, comes the moment of empathic strategy—this poem, in fact, turns on one powerful question. Here are the last three lines:

> Still haunted by my first devils,
> Alone and sick, lying in a foreign house,
> I try to read. Which one of us is absent?

One of the reclaimed poems, "The Figure on the Far Side," provides another example. As with much of Jane Cooper's work, excerpting is difficult, so here is the entire poem:

> Once it was my brother on
> the far side of the chessboard.
> His lean ribcage puffed with
> concentration, his lower
> lip clenched in his huge second
> teeth, he whistled slightly; he
> let out his breath as he pounced.
>
> And I was so stupid that
> twisting with discomfort I
> answered Capablanca's
> fifteen-minute pauses with
> tears! arias! any old pawn
> rushed out in a fury to
> die and get the game over!
>
> I must be the only one
> alive, I start, who gave up
> chess at seven. . . . But the
> young doctor waits. What if he

laughs? Shouldn't he care? Damn you,
the silence ticks, how can you
nurse such secrets and keep still?

The reconstruction of the brother in the first stanza and the way
the line breaks (enjambed and falling with deliberate awkwardness
after prepositions or pronouns) contribute to the sense of the
speaker "twisting with discomfort" are among the pleasures of this
poem. But my reason to quote it is the last four lines, in which the
"game" changes along with the "opposing" figure. The implications
of the comparison multiply and complicate themselves even as we
realize where the speaker now is. And it seems to me that the mo-
ment is given to us in such a way that we are not meant to take it
in all at once. The last sentence could be read is if it were three:
"Damn you. The silence ticks. How can you nurse such secrets and
keep still?" That is how I first read it, believing that the speaker is
silently addressing the young doctor. After living with the poem for
a few readings, I came to believe the primary reading is that the
silence is addressing the poem's speaker and asking the final ques-
tion.

What is remarkable about the last stanza is how finely it is con-
trolled. I am sure that the poet means me to hold the two interpre-
tations up and choose one—and yet not choose. For we know the
silent doctor does have his secrets, as the speaker has hers, as we all
have. The possibility of that second reading augments the transfor-
mation of brother to doctor. Who is here? "Which one of us is ab-
sent?"

Two new poems much later in *The Flashboat* provide a final ex-
ample of what I've been calling a strategy of empathy. "Scattered
Words for Emily Dickinson" and "S. Eliason 66: *Double Portrait of
Emily Dickinson and the Rev. Charles Wadsworth*" are on facing pages,
and in themselves form a kind of double portrait of Eliason and her
painting. Here is the first:

SCATTERED WORDS FOR EMILY DICKINSON

I

Inside the crate, dark
as corn in its sheath   sheet lightning

2

This painting was made in Iowa
under the gold sky of the Great Plains.
In her Puritan white dress
in his fiberboard suit
(the rev. family man, from Philadelphia)
at the conservator door   they
start forth

flashbulbs!

ochre   orange   flame   black   black   white

Brilliant Pioneer Roots   and
difficult geography the face of a friend:
(brilliant) notes from the painter's (my friend's) catalogue
(difficult) notes from the painter's (a pioneer's) catalogue

3

So the stolid-looking veteran
(G.I. Bill, History of the Language)
told me, speaking of combat:
            In the least space
            between two bodies
            there is room
            for mystery

And since excerpting, again, seems a disservice (it leaves these po-
ems in particular behind), I'll quote the second poem of the pair
likewise in its entirety:

S. Eliason 66: *Double Portrait of Emily Dickinson*
and the Rev. Charles Wadsworth

She is just leaving the room.
He fades to a china cup.

Velocity fraught with gold,
with *menace of light,* atomic secrets—
An aroused skin opens over the Great Plains.
October leaves rain down.

Corn in conflagration!
The great retreats of the Civil War!
Marriage in conflagration!

Years—an empty canvas.
She scrawls across radiant space

E . . . I . . . SON! *I made this.* The date.
Name within name.

The empathy is more complicated here: poet, painter, and two
historical figures perform a complex dance in these poems, consid-
ered either singly or together. Names overlap in a greater sense than
that of recurring letters in "Emily Dickinson" and "Eliason." Who's
present, absent? And yet the sense of control is again apparent: words
have been "scattered" with great care. Some images occur in both
poems: corn and sky, plains and fire. And space, dangerously radiant
in "Double Portrait" and intimately dangerous in "Scattered Words."
The parallel imagery makes these two poems almost two versions
of one thing, or of the painting.

Despite its chronological arrangement, *The Flashboat* rises to a
finale, one that has much to do with the idea—or rather the habit
of mind, the practice—of empathy. The last book collected here,
Green Notebook, Winter Road, moves through four sections, the final
one containing two poems in which Cooper's voice is raised in
chorus with those of other women who dedicated themselves to
their art, first Georgia O'Keeffe (*"The Winter Road"*) and then
Willa Cather.

"The Winter Road" begins with the figure of O'Keeffe in the
second person ("You stand on a ridge facing silence / You lift your
brush"). It then moves closer, describing the landscape as if seen
through the painter's eyes ("Rib cage of cliffs // . . . It can all be
told in color and light and line") and introducing italicized lines
and phrases that are clearly quotes from the painter (*"even the soft
earth greens // Clarify"*). And then, with the quiet intensity so char-
acteristic of Cooper, pronouns and italics shift. Here is the last sec-
tion of "The Winter Road":

Where I have been
Where I have been is of no importance
To live to be a hundred is of no importance

only *what I have done* with it
 But we love the particular

Where I was born
Where I was born is of no importance
         torn shoe, nursing mouth, patchwork-cushioned chair
         still rocking quietly in the light wind
         of a late summer evening of some life

Nor *how I have lived*
with a handful of rocks
a wooden bodhisattva in a niche
a black door
and the continuous great adventure of the sky

Only what I have made of it
what I have been able to finish
To live to be a hundred is of no importance
This landscape is not human
I was meant to take nothing away

I read this passage as a duet, marked by the introduction of the
"I" not in italics. Of course it is still O'Keeffe—the images of chair,
shoe, black door and sky tell us that even as they answer the first
stanza's "love [of] the particular." But the pronoun in Roman type
has modulated from "you" to "I," and that signifies both a closeness
(the speaker is here, not addressing from a distance) and an inclusion
(not a substitution) of the poet's own voice. It is a subtle but moving
effect, in accord with the calm poignancy of the poem's content.

The last poem of *The Flashboat* likewise extends community to
communion. "Vocation: A Life" is longer, a sectioned poem, subti-
tled "Suite Based on Four Words from Willa Cather"; the words
turn out to be "desire," "romance," "possession," and—surprisingly—
"unfurnishing." The poem moves through Cather's books speaking
to and about her, and often through her characters. It reconstructs
Cather from her own constructions, and while "Vocation: A Life"
creates a more comprehensive portrait than the one in the first
poem discussed here, the two poems perhaps derive from some-
thing of the same impulse. (In "For My Mother in Her First Illness,"
you remember, the young mother has to be "reconstruct[ed] . . .
feature by feature.")

And while "Vocation" doesn't mix the voices of the poet and her projection in quite the way that "The Winter Road" does, it achieves a similar effect. For Cather is cast in the same light in which Cooper presents herself in the essay "Nothing Has Been Used in the Manufacture of This Poetry That Could Have Been Used in the Manufacture of Bread." If autobiography is not poetry, neither is biography. What Cooper creates in "Vocation: A Life" is the "rearrangement" of the details of a life to make it "more true," to make it a poem. "THE PROFESSOR'S HOUSE *is . . . the most personal of Willa Cather's novels,*" Cooper quotes "valiant Edith Lewis" toward the end of "Vocation," and then adds "therefore, not autobiographical." Making a life, constructing it by arranging words on a page, is Cather's vocation and Cooper's.

> When we try to sum up a lifetime, events cease to matter
> just as, in the end, a novel's
> plot does not matter
> What we came away with was never written down
> *Vibration, overtone, timbre,* a fragrance as distinct
> as that of an old walled garden . . . *The text is not there—*
> *but something was there, all the same,* some intimacy,
> all that is needed
> in a vigorous, rich speaking voice
>
> [Your] *secret?*
> *It is every artist's secret.* Your secret
> was *passion*

Appreciating the mysteriousness of art—the "something" that cannot be found in the text but that nevertheless rises from it—requires, it seems to me, the empathy that I have been describing, even if it is not an explicit subject. That Jane Cooper uses it explicitly at times is evidence of how central it is to her work.

Given that *The Flashboat* is a product of so many years of work, a comment on style is in order. While one can see the development of an individual voice across these pages, what is most striking is the stylistic versatility. The book opens with a sestina, followed by poems that make agile use of meter and rhyme. Soon Cooper is employing irregular stanzas, dropped lines and other free verse techniques. But this is not a case in which a young poet tries on a number of different styles to see which works best and then settles in to make good use of the possibilities of the chosen style. This is a restless and inventive mind continuing to experiment, probing for the most advantageous way to deal with the occasion of each poem. So, for example, even late in the book there are poems in quatrains and tercets; and prose pieces appear only a few pages before the spare poetry considered above.

One of the shorter prose pieces, "How Can I Speak for Her?," is a piecing together, from stories told in the family, of an encounter between the speaker's great-great-grandmother and a freed slave a few years after the Civil War. It is extraordinarily powerful, and it shows Cooper recognizing a limit beyond which her imagination should not reach. For at the understated but inherently dramatic climax, the poet interrupts herself with the title's question. While her empathy urges her to speak for the former slave, another of Cooper's habits of mind—a rigorous moral inspection of herself—causes her to stop. She gives us everything she can, and the tact of appropriate restraint.

The Flashboat is clearly the work of a poet who is not afraid to take risks, either in terms of style or of the imaginative leap of empathy. This characteristic is captured with lyric economy in the title poem, a compelling dream-sequence in which the speaker describes abandoning a sinking ship in the dark of night:

> The crew makes ready the boats. One near me, broad but shallow,
> looks safe, women are urged, the captain will be in charge.
> Far down now: a trough. A smaller dory rocks
> in and out of our lights; black fists grip the oars.
> Room only for six—we will
> all need to row.
> For a moment I hesitate, worrying about my defective blood.
> A rope ladder drops over. My voice with its crunch of bone
> wakes me: *I choose*
> *the flashboat!*
> > work,
> > > the starry waters

The speaker wakes herself with her own voice as she chooses the smaller boat, the boat that requires work, instead of the shallow vessel under the captain's charge to which women are urged; she wants to put her hands to work with the black hands, to take responsibility for her own fate, and she wants these things more than she wants safety. The metaphors, though abundant, are unobtrusive. The dream-speak neologism "flashboat" suggests both the moments of clarity that illuminate individual poems and the buoyant craft that carries the writer forward. It is our good fortune that many years ago Jane Cooper chose as she did, for *The Flashboat* is a book that enlightens and sustains us.

DAVID RIGSBEE

The Flashboat
Poems Collected and Reclaimed

Poetry of a higher order courts two kinds of difficulty. The first is
formal, connected with the degrees of ellipsis, or leaving out, that a
poem can sustain and still be subject to understanding. This sort has
been long thought—wrongly—applicable to some early New York
School poetry (and *all* language poetry) but is most rightly applied
to poems with submerged narratives, poems whose effects are con-
spicuous even as their occasions are more or less invisible. The sec-
ond sort of difficulty is encountered in poems registering deep
struggles that by and by the poems come to embody as well. When
this happens, such a poem becomes emblematic of the value (for
the poem) and dignity (for the poet) that may accrue in the struggle
for significance—even if insignificance is the result. The assumed
"depth" implies hidden forces by which one may posit anything
from God to history to psychic wrestling. The struggle takes place
below the urge, and the resulting poem is both a description of the
struggle and one of its forms. Its victories are not mere lyric victo-
ries: they may also be real gains. As a result, the poem collapses the
contested ground between imagination and reality. It is therefore
the kind of difficulty often associated with wonder, the flip side, you
might say, of bafflement.

Jane Cooper's poems are of the second, more metaphysical sort.
The Flashboat: Poems Collected and Reclaimed maps fifty years of
shrewd reflection and dogged engagement. While descending into
fields of struggle may run counter to post-modernity's infinite re-
gressions, where no buck stops, Jane Cooper's poems incorporate
encounters. And that's not all: they acknowledge the force of the
question whether the lived world a) is atoms all the way down or b)
may be conceived somehow free of the dictatorship of matter—as
with history, God, traditions, Zeitgeists, or mindsets.

Cooper's first poems are hyperalert to historical context. As she
puts it in a speech, "Poetry is a way of giving people more life, a

more vivid awareness of the exact moment they are living through—first a sensuous [sic] awareness, then a historical one." While it may be the province of the "I" to have experiences in the here and now, it is only part of a sequence, the end of which is judgment. While her early poems hash through the difficulties of relationships (a recurring theme), they never have to do so without keeping one eye on the times. The poet knows better than to give sexuality, friendship, domesticity, or the artist's quandaries stand-alone billing. A World War II poem ("The Faithful") suggests this inescapable doubling:

> What if last night I was the one who lay dead
> While the dead burned beside me
> Trembling with passionate pity
> At my blameless life and shaking its flamelike head?

It is revealing to contrast Cooper's response to the Second World War with the famous responses of her male poet colleagues, whose publishable psychic scars helped form a new personal discourse seemingly unavailable in the 1930s. Cooper's reaction was an attempt to triangulate a different set of problems: non-participation, guilt, and responsibility. For instance, her feminism would be partly colored by the grim absorption of the war years and the idealistic aftermath when the Marshall Plan seemed, among other things, a metaphor for the American renewal of Euro-culture. Clustering around cultural centers herself—Vassar, New York, Princeton, Oxford—Cooper had imbibed the prevailing notion of a noble cause, a nostalgia not uncommon for a girl reared in the South, but now sanctified with the halo of Einstein's hair. In "After the Bomb Tests," scientific saintliness becomes the object of artistic query, just as the scientist's object (or fetish)—the atom—has become a source of study and means to a higher end. Here, with Kepler standing in for Einstein, the crossover between artistic and scientific inquiry suggests that their opposing alchemies are often complicit in their desire for power:

> The atom bellies like a cauliflower,
> Expands, expands, shoots up again, expands
> Into ecclesiastical curves and towers
> We pray to with our cupped and empty hands.
> . . .
> Could one harmony hold

The sum of private freedom like a cup?

. . .

> Kepler, curious, rose,
> Started to cross himself—then like a lover
> Or virgin artist gave himself to his power.

As *The Flashboat* makes plain, running parallel with the poet's
attempts to come to grips with history are her attempts to measure
private trials—the disillusionments at ten o'clock, in Stevens's
phrase. These include not only the artist's dilemma between work
and private life but also the prior matter of health (Cooper had all
her life suffered from a reduced immune system):

> My body knows it will never bear children.
> What can I say to my body now,
> this used violin?
> Every night it cries out strenuously
> from its secret cave.

Not only the body's pilgrimage but also its rhetorical representa-
tion becomes an issue. Cooper speaks of an artistic affinity for
theme-and-variation approaches to writing about experience, and
over time these have acquired sufficient irony to pack, in their turn,
abundant cautions when needed to constrain occasional excesses:

> Yes, I'm the lady he wrote the sonnets to.
> I can tell you how it was
> And where the books lie, biographies and his
> Famous later versions now collected
> In one volume for lovers. (You
> Can never really analyze his method
>
> If you only read those.)

By mid-career Cooper had made the cartographer's sense of in-
telligible distortions a part of her own artistic awareness. Accuracy
is not the only compliment fidelity pays to art: Mercator's projec-
tions make coordinates too, although they occur in no existential
realms other than ones we may be said to imagine. In Cooper's
rhetoric, the distance between what was necessary to endure then,
as opposed to now, is equivalent to the difference between Merca-
tor's gigantic Greenland and the much more modest island offered

by Planet Earth. Therefore, because perspectives vary, the possibility of human acknowledgment-across-time (and its emanation, forgiveness) looms large. In one of several pieces devoted to the modalities and endurance of disability, benediction becomes benefaction in lines that recall Whitman:

> Mercy on Maryanne who through a hole beneath her collarbone
>   drinks the life-preserving fluid, while in her arm
> another IV tube drips something green. "It never affects me," she
>   says, "I'm fortunate."
> She has Crohn's and rheumatoid arthritis and now osteoporosis, as
>   well as no gamma globulin
> as we all have no gamma globulin, or at least not enough. Mercy
>   on Aaron,
> her son, who at fifteen has Hodgkins and arthritis and no gamma
>   globulin, who is out of school
> just for the moment. "He's so bright," the doctor says, "he'll make
>   it up." But of course
> you never (as I remember) quite make it up . . .

The world mapped by desire is also a world where distinctions between safety and participation do not arise. But witness—the taking-in—replaces projection—the thrusting out; not surprisingly, the poet comes to question the tools of her art, as in "In a Room with Picassos":

> . . . I can stand and stand
> In front of canvas and artistic paraphernalia
> But nothing there will answer me with pride:
> *I am the exact shade of shame and desire.*
> *Your justification in the face of his*
> *Simple indifference to simple fire.*
> *I am the offering which always moves*
> *Anyone, no matter how far away he is from love.*

Cooper is admirable in the degree to which she accepts resistance of people and things to reductive meanings, even when these might only provide gentle rubrics and consolations. Unconsoled, she can say, as in the speak of "My friend" [sic], *"But I don't know,* she broke off, / *whether I'm making myself clear . . ."* The hesitation here clears more ground than a legion of necessary fictions. It is not clear, in one of several poems involving historical personages (Emily Dickinson, Georgia O'Keeffe, Willa Cather) what led Rosa Luxemburg to extol, on the one hand, the glories of war, and on the other to tender beauties of the natural world. But these contraries stand for the poet's capacity to accept the spectrum that begins with mere inconsistencies and ends with solid contradictions as saying something worthwhile about the world:

> *It's no use telling myself I am not responsible for all the hungry little larks*
> *in the world. Logic does not help*
> Never mind, we shall live   shall live
> through grand events
> Have patience
> Thus passing out of my cell in all directions
> are fine threads connecting me
> with thousands of birds and beasts

The poet knows that often contradiction favors truth more closely than logic, and this knowledge situates her poems with a familiarity among paradoxes that the mind rejects, although the body never stops squirming through their medium.

Beyond these frank and wise poems of acknowledgment—poems one feels the result of infinite winnowing—she has chosen to include several prose narratives, the last of which is a memoir of, and meditation on, a serious childhood illness. Here is a world where contingency, like original sin, preconditions all subsequent states and consciousness. But what kind of mooring is contingency when we must both set out from it and abide by it? Cooper's poems—trusty, spare, hopeful, yet beautifully deflationary—log the rigor of this ultimate paradox.

L. R. BERGER

The Last Poem

> . . . the Queen Mary is sinking.
> . . . A smaller dory rocks
> in and out of our lights . . .
> . . . we will
> all need to row.

("The Flashboat," 144)

Between your question and my answer, we sat still and tall as two mountains. I can't remember the weather outside your late October window. You said, "I don't understand what is happening now," half statement, half fearful inquiry. Then I kept the promise we made to each other, the truth for when it was time.

"Oh, the price of love," you said, tending to me all tear-fall now and trembling, and reached across the tray table asking, "Can you spare a hand?" "How long do they say I have?" Then lunch arrived though you were no longer eating. Surveying your plate, you flashed a wry smile, "Did you ever imagine we'd be having this conversation over an egg salad sandwich?"

Talking about dying was enough to inspire your nap, and while you were sleeping in your chair, I remembered the story you told about the time you were a young woman at death's door. Looking down from a great height at your poor body on the hospital bed, you could hear the nurses and doctors whispering, bowed over you. Then you remembered you hadn't yet been kissed, and described the strenuousness required to climb back down into your body, reclaiming your life.

On that last afternoon, the bushes were burning outside your window packed with song sparrows. John, the aide you loved for his kindness, came to lift you one final time into bed from your chair. You were unsteady in his arms but he reassured you, "Jane, you can do this. This is just your last poem."

You slept awhile, your breathing labored, and then you began to row. That's the only way there is to describe it: your hands and arms rowing with great effort in the air, what would have been strong backstrokes in any dory. I offered you my hands, and feeling for them with closed eyes, you gripped them each like oars and went on rowing. So we were both rowing, your groaning timed to rounding each arduous stroke, as if pressing into the weight of a choppy sea. You were going; you were not to be taken.

You had rowed beyond words hours before, so I didn't expect you to come all the way back to answer. But when the sounds of your laboring sharpened, I asked, "Jane, are you in pain?" Your arms stilled then, and your everyday eyes opened, piercingly tender and clear. "It's not exactly like that," you said. Then closed your eyes to journey the rest of the way.

Contributors

Pamela Alexander has published four collections of poetry, most recently *Slow Fire*. Her nonfiction has appeared in *Denver Quarterly* and *Cimarron Review*. She taught writing at M.I.T. and Oberlin College.

Kazim Ali teaches at Oberlin College and is the author of twenty books in various genres, including most recently *Inquisition*, a collection of poetry.

Maggie Anderson is the author of five books of poetry, most recently *Dear All*. She is Professor Emerita from Kent State University and lives in Asheville, NC.

L. R. Berger's *The Unexpected Aviary* received the Jane Kenyon Award for Outstanding Book of Poetry. With Kamal Boullatta, she assisted in the translation from Arabic of *Beginnings* by Adonis.

Ned Balbo's books include *Upcycling Paumanok*. Among his awards are the Poets' Prize, the Ernest Sandeen Prize, the Richard Wilbur Award, and a National Endowment for the Arts Translation grant.

Celia Bland's poetry collections include *Cherokee Road Kill*, *Soft Box*, and *Madonna Comix*. She teaches at Bard College.

Lee Briccetti is the long-time director of Poets House in New York City. Her books of poems include *Day Mark* (2005) and *Blue Guide* (2018).

Marilyn Chin is a poet, story writer, translator, and social activist. Her newest book is *A Portrait of the Self as Nation: New and Selected Poems* (2018). She lives in San Diego.

Martha Collins has published nine books of poetry, including *Night Unto Night* (2018), *Admit One: An American Scrapbook* (2016), and *Day Unto Day* (2014). She lives in Cambridge, Massachusetts.

Jenny Factor lectures on poetry at Antioch University and the California Institute of Technology. Her book *Unraveling at the Name* was a Lambda Award finalist.

Beatrix Gates, as a fellow at the Huntington Library, worked on "Good Seeing: A Poem of the Full Sky." Her collections include *In the Open* and *Dos*.

Eve Grubin is the author of *Morning Prayer* and *The House of Our First Loving*. She teaches at NYU in London.

Eric Gudas is the author of *Best Western and Other Poems* (2010).

Rachel Hadas's most recent works, a verse translation of Euripides' two Iphigenia plays and *Poems for Camilla*, a new collection of poetry, were published in 2018.

Marie Howe is the author of four books of poetry, most recently *Magdalene*. She was New York State Poet from 2012–2014. She teaches at Sarah Lawrence College.

Galway Kinnell (1927–2014) published numerous collections of poetry, including the 1982 *Selected Poems*, which won both a Pulitzer Prize and a National Book Award.

Jan Heller Levi's most recent books are *Orphan* and, co-edited with Christoph Keller, *We're On: A June Jordan Reader*.

Philip Levine (1928–2015) published more than twenty volumes of poetry during his lifetime, and served as United States Poet Laureate in 2011.

Thomas Lux (1946–2017) was the author of fourteen books of poetry, including *Split Horizon*, which won the Kingsley Tufts Poetry Award.

Gail Mazur's collections include *Forbidden City; Figures in a Landscape; Zeppo's First Wife: New & Selected Poems*; and *They Can't Take That Away from Me*, a finalist for the National Book Award.

Carley Moore is the author of a collection of essays, *16 Pills;* a novel, *The Not Wives*; a poetry chapbook, *Portal Poem*; and the young adult novel *The Stalker Chronicles*.

Kevin Prufer is the author of several poetry collections, most recently *How He Loved Them* (2018), *Churches* (2014), and *In a Beautiful Country* (2011). He is Professor of English in the University of Houston's Creative Writing Program.

David Rigsbee is the author of eleven full-length collections, including *School of the Americas* (2012) and *This Much I Can Tell You* (2017), and *Not Alone in My Dancing: Essays and Reviews* (2016).

Clare Rossini's third collection of poems, *Lingo*, was published in 2006. She is co-editing, with Benjamin S. Grossberg, *The Poetry of Capital*, an anthology of poetry assessing the contemporary American relationship with money, due out in 2019.

Lisa Sack attended Princeton University and holds an MFA from Columbia University's Writing Division. She is currently a yoga therapist in Brooklyn, New York.

Lee Sharkey is the author most recently of *Walking Backwards* and *Calendars of Fire*. Her recognitions include the Ballymaloe Poetry Prize and the Abraham Sutzkever Centennial Prize.

Lisa Sperber teaches writing at the University of California, Davis. She has co-edited a book of interviews with composition teacher-scholars, *Teachers on the Edge* (2017).

Stephen Tapscott is the author of four books of poems; he works at M.I.T and lives in Cambridge, Massachusetts.

Lynne Thompson is the author of *Beg No Pardon* and *Start With A Small Guitar*. Her forthcoming poetry collection is the winner of the 2018 Marsh Hawk Press Poetry Prize.

Lee Upton's most recent books are *Visitations: Stories* and *Bottle the Bottles the Bottles the Bottles: Poems.*

Jean Valentine is the author of many books of poetry, and taught for a number of years at Sarah Lawrence College with Jane Cooper.

James Wright (1927–1980) published ten volumes of poetry during his lifetime, including the Pulitzer Prize-winning *Collected Poems* (1971).

Patricia Younge is Professor Emeritus of English, University of Houston, and for many years has been a Willa Cather scholar and specialist in the 1920s. Her publications also include studies of American and European women auto racers of the interwar era.

Printed and bound by CPI Group (UK) Ltd, Croydon, CR0 4YY

09/06/2025

14686091-0001